# THE ULTIMATE AIR FRYER COOKBOOK for Beginners 2024

1900 Days of Easy, Delicious, and Budget-Friendly Recipes for Healthy Homemade Meals

Elizabeth Williams

**All Rights Reserved.**

The contents of this book may not be reproduced, copied or transmitted without the direct written permission of the author or publisher. Under no circumstances will the publisher or the author be held responsible or liable for any damage, compensation or pecuniary loss arising directly or indirectly from the information contained in this book.

Legal notice. This book is protected by copyright. It is intended for personal use only. You may not modify, distribute, sell, use, quote or paraphrase any part or content of this book without the consent of the author or publisher.

**Notice Of Disclaimer.**

Please note that the information in this document is intended for educational and entertainment purposes only. Every effort has been made to provide accurate, up-to-date, reliable and complete information. No warranty of any kind is declared or implied. The reader acknowledges that the author does not engage in the provision of legal, financial, medical or professional advice. The content in this book has been obtained from a variety of sources. Please consult a licensed professional before attempting any of the techniques described in this book. By reading this document, the reader agrees that in no event shall the author be liable for any direct or indirect damages, including but not limited to errors, omissions or inaccuracies, resulting from the use of the information in this document.

# CONTENTS

**INTRODUCTION** ..................................................... 1

## Bread And Breakfast ............................. 3

Bacon Puff Pastry Pinwheels ............................................ 3
Mascarpone Iced Cinnamon Rolls ................................... 3
Apricot-cheese Mini Pies ................................................. 3
Lime Muffins ................................................................... 4
Cinnamon Banana Bread With Pecans ........................... 4
Tri-color Frittata .............................................................. 4
Cheddar & Sausage Tater Tots ....................................... 5
Cheesy Egg Popovers ..................................................... 5
Chia Seed Banana Bread ................................................ 5
Mushroom & Cavolo Nero Egg Muffins ........................ 5
Chili Hash Browns .......................................................... 6
Egg And Sausage Crescent Rolls .................................... 6
Herby Parmesan Pita ...................................................... 7
Oat & Nut Granola ......................................................... 7
Mediterranean Granola ................................................... 7
Cinnamon Biscuit Rolls ................................................... 8
Morning Loaded Potato Skins ........................................ 8
Colorful French Toast Sticks ........................................... 8
Honey Donuts ................................................................. 9
Thai Turkey Sausage Patties ........................................... 9

## Fish And Seafood Recipes ........ 10

Coconut-shrimp Po' Boys .............................................. 10
Cajun-seasoned Shrimp ................................................ 10
Super Crunchy Flounder Fillets .................................... 10
Crispy Sweet-and-sour Cod Fillets ............................... 11
Lime Halibut Parcels ..................................................... 11
Saucy Shrimp ................................................................ 11
Shrimp Al Pesto ............................................................ 12
Spicy Fish Street Tacos With Sriracha Slaw ................. 12
Basil Crab Cakes With Fresh Salad .............................. 12
Fish And "chips" ........................................................... 13
Speedy Shrimp Paella ................................................... 13
French Grouper Nicoise ................................................ 13
Nutty Shrimp With Amaretto Glaze ............................. 14
Fish Tacos With Jalapeño-lime Sauce .......................... 14
Buttered Swordfish Steaks ............................................ 15

Perfect Soft-shelled Crabs ............................................. 15
Home-style Fish Sticks .................................................. 15
Sweet Potato–wrapped Shrimp .................................... 15
Tilapia Al Pesto ............................................................. 16
Flounder Fillets ............................................................. 16

## Beef, Pork & Lamb Recipes ..... 17

Lamb Chops .................................................................. 17
Barbecue-style London Broil ........................................ 17
Canadian-style Rib Eye Steak ...................................... 17
Chinese-style Lamb Chops ........................................... 18
Stuffed Pork Chops ....................................................... 18
Pretzel-coated Pork Tenderloin ..................................... 18
Chorizo & Veggie Bake ................................................ 19
Greek Pork Chops ......................................................... 19
Sloppy Joes ................................................................... 19
Crispy Pierogi With Kielbasa And Onions ................... 20
Lamb Meatballs With Quick Tomato Sauce ................ 20
Honey Mesquite Pork Chops ........................................ 21
Sausage-cheese Calzone ............................................... 21
Pork Cutlets With Aloha Salsa ..................................... 22
Tender Steak With Salsa Verde .................................... 22
Peachy Pork Chops ....................................................... 22
Barbecue-style Beef Cube Steak .................................. 23
Original Köttbullar ........................................................ 23
Classic Beef Meatballs .................................................. 23
Pork Tenderloin With Apples & Celery ........................ 24

## Appetizers And Snacks ............... 24

Tomato & Garlic Roasted Potatoes .............................. 24
Sweet-and-salty Pretzels ............................................... 24
Mediterranean Potato Skins ......................................... 25
Spicy Chicken And Pepper Jack Cheese Bites ............. 25
Beef Steak Sliders ......................................................... 26
Hot Avocado Fries ........................................................ 26
Spiced Nuts ................................................................... 26
Prosciutto Polenta Rounds ........................................... 27
Fried" Pickles With Homemade Ranch ....................... 27
Zucchini Fritters ............................................................ 27
Fiery Cheese Sticks ....................................................... 28

Asian-style Shrimp Toast .................................................. 28
Country Wings ..................................................................... 28
Cheesy Zucchini Chips ..................................................... 29
Crab Toasts ......................................................................... 29
Artichoke-spinach Dip ..................................................... 29
Avocado Fries With Quick Salsa Fresca ....................... 29
Greek Street Tacos ............................................................ 30
Polenta Fries With Chili-lime Mayo ............................... 30
Parmesan Pizza Nuggets .................................................. 31

## Poultry Recipes ............................................................ 31

Chicken Breasts Wrapped In Bacon ............................. 31
Chicken Salad With Roasted Vegetables .................... 32
Chicken Meatballs With A Surprise ............................... 32
Chicken Pigs In Blankets ................................................. 32
Thai Turkey And Zucchini Meatballs ............................. 33
Chicago-style Turkey Meatballs .................................... 33
Chicken Skewers ............................................................... 33
Chicken Souvlaki Gyros .................................................. 34
Fennel & Chicken Ratatouille ......................................... 34
Favorite Fried Chicken Wings ........................................ 34
Coconut Chicken With Apricot-ginger Sauce ........... 35
Philly Chicken Cheesesteak Stromboli ......................... 35
German Chicken Frikadellen .......................................... 36
Spinach & Turkey Meatballs .......................................... 36
Spicy Black Bean Turkey Burgers With Cumin-avocado Spread ............................................................... 36
Southern-fried Chicken Livers ....................................... 37
Crispy "fried" Chicken ..................................................... 37
Crispy Chicken Parmesan ............................................... 38
Maple Bacon Wrapped Chicken Breasts .................... 38
Jerk Chicken Drumsticks ................................................. 39

## Vegetable Side Dishes Recipes ........................... 39

Zucchini Fries .................................................................... 39
Hawaiian Brown Rice ...................................................... 40
Asparagus Fries ................................................................. 40
Italian Breaded Eggplant Rounds ................................. 40
Lemony Green Bean Sauté ............................................ 40
Grits Casserole .................................................................. 41
Toasted Choco-nuts ........................................................ 41
Dijon Roasted Purple Potatoes ..................................... 41
Roasted Garlic And Thyme Tomatoes ........................ 42
Tuna Platter ....................................................................... 42
Cholula Onion Rings ....................................................... 42

Spicy Fried Green Beans ................................................. 43
Garlicky Brussels Sprouts ............................................... 43
Broccoli Au Gratin ............................................................ 43
Mediterranean Roasted Vegetables ............................. 44
Fried Eggplant Balls ......................................................... 44
Roman Artichokes ............................................................ 44
Buttery Stuffed Tomatoes ............................................... 45
Honey-roasted Parsnips .................................................. 45
Roasted Peppers With Balsamic Vinegar And Basil .. 45

## Sandwiches And Burgers Recipes ....................... 46

Chili Cheese Dogs ............................................................ 46
Chicken Apple Brie Melt ................................................. 46
Chicken Spiedies .............................................................. 47
Eggplant Parmesan Subs ................................................ 47
Provolone Stuffed Meatballs ......................................... 48
Salmon Burgers ................................................................. 48
Thanksgiving Turkey Sandwiches ................................. 48
Chicken Gyros ................................................................... 49
Mexican Cheeseburgers .................................................. 49
Dijon Thyme Burgers ....................................................... 50
White Bean Veggie Burgers ........................................... 51
Black Bean Veggie Burgers ............................................ 51
Perfect Burgers ................................................................. 52
Sausage And Pepper Heros ........................................... 52
Crunchy Falafel Balls ...................................................... 52
Chicken Club Sandwiches .............................................. 53
Inside Out Cheeseburgers .............................................. 53
Philly Cheesesteak Sandwiches .................................... 54
Chicken Saltimbocca Sandwiches ................................ 54
Inside-out Cheeseburgers .............................................. 54

## Vegetarian Recipes .................................................... 55

Party Giant Nachos .......................................................... 55
Black Bean Stuffed Potato Boats .................................. 55
Creamy Broccoli & Mushroom Casserole ................... 56
Thyme Lentil Patties ........................................................ 56
Asparagus, Mushroom And Cheese Soufflés ............ 56
Spicy Sesame Tempeh Slaw With Peanut Dressing 57
Gorgeous Jalapeño Poppers ......................................... 57
Pinto Bean Casserole ...................................................... 58
Roasted Vegetable Pita Pizza ........................................ 58
Falafel ................................................................................. 58
Roasted Veggie Bowls ..................................................... 59

Rigatoni With Roasted Onions, Fennel, Spinach And Lemon Pepper Ricotta ................................................. 59
Vietnamese Gingered Tofu ............................................. 59
Vegetarian Paella ........................................................... 60
Pineapple & Veggie Souvlaki ......................................... 60
Garlicky Roasted Mushrooms ........................................ 60
Lentil Fritters .................................................................. 61
Healthy Living Mushroom Enchiladas ............................ 61
Mushroom Bolognese Casserole ................................... 62
Honey Pear Chips .......................................................... 62

## Desserts And Sweets .................................................. 62
Giant Buttery Oatmeal Cookie ....................................... 62
Strawberry Donut Bites .................................................. 63
Apple Dumplings ............................................................ 63
Guilty Chocolate Cookies ............................................... 64
Donut Holes ................................................................... 64
Almond-roasted Pears ................................................... 64
Pear And Almond Biscotti Crumble ................................ 65
Fruity Oatmeal Crisp ...................................................... 65
Chewy Coconut Cake .................................................... 65
Keto Cheesecake Cups ................................................. 66
Mango-chocolate Custard .............................................. 66
Blueberry Crisp .............................................................. 66
Sugared Pizza Dough Dippers With Raspberry Cream Cheese Dip ............................................................ 67
Holiday Peppermint Cake .............................................. 67
Famous Chocolate Lava Cake ....................................... 67
Sweet Potato Pie Rolls .................................................. 68
Banana-lemon Bars ....................................................... 68
Chocolate Cake .............................................................. 68
Fried Twinkies ................................................................ 69
Holiday Pear Crumble .................................................... 69

## INDEX .......................................................................... 70

# INTRODUCTION

🔍 Have you recently acquired an air fryer and are eager to explore its full potential?

💭 Wondering how to create delicious, healthy meals without breaking the bank?

🕐 Struggling to find time for cooking nutritious homemade dishes?

Look no further! "The Ultimate Air Fryer Cookbook for Beginners 2024" is here to revolutionize your cooking experience!

✹ What makes this cookbook your essential kitchen companion? ✹

☑ 1900 Days of Culinary Inspiration: Never run out of ideas with our extensive collection of recipes that will keep your meals exciting for over 5 years!

☑ Beginner-Friendly Approach: Each recipe features clear, step-by-step instructions, making it easy for even novice cooks to create impressive dishes.

☑ Budget-Conscious Cooking: Discover how to make mouthwatering meals using affordable, easily accessible ingredients that won't strain your wallet.

☑ Time-Saving Solutions: Most recipes can be prepared in 30 minutes or less, perfect for busy individuals and families.

☑ Health-Focused Recipes: Enjoy your favorite fried foods with a fraction of the oil, without compromising on taste or texture.

📚 Inside this comprehensive cookbook, you'll find:

🔍 Energizing breakfast options to start your day right

🍽 Nutritious lunch ideas for work or home

🍗 Family-friendly dinner recipes that will please even the pickiest eaters

🥨 Crowd-pleasing snacks and appetizers for any occasion

🍰 Guilt-free desserts to satisfy your sweet tooth

But that's not all! We've also included:

- Expert tips and tricks for mastering your air fryer

- A guide to adapting traditional recipes for air frying

- Nutritional information for each dish

- Ingredient substitution suggestions for various dietary needs

🍳 With "The Ultimate Air Fryer Cookbook for Beginners 2024," you'll transform your kitchen into a hub of quick, healthy, and delicious meals. Say goodbye to expensive takeout and hello to homemade goodness that's kind to your health and your budget.

🎉🎉🎉 Ready to embark on your air frying journey? Click "Buy Now" now and unlock a world of culinary possibilities! Whether you're cooking for one or feeding a family, this cookbook will be your go-to resource for easy, delicious, and budget-friendly meals that will have everyone asking for seconds. Don't miss out on this opportunity to revolutionize your cooking and enjoy healthier, homemade meals every day of the week! 🎉🎉🎉

# Bread And Breakfast

## Bacon Puff Pastry Pinwheels

**Servings: 8 | Prep Time: 15 Minutes | Cooking Time: 10 Minutes**

### Ingredients:

- 1 sheet puff pastry
- 2 tablespoons maple syrup
- ¼ cup brown sugar
- 8 slices bacon (not thick cut)
- Coarsely cracked black pepper
- Vegetable oil

### Directions:

1. On a lightly floured surface, roll puff pastry into a 25x28cm square. Cut into 8 strips.
2. Brush pastry with maple syrup and sprinkle with brown sugar, leaving 5cm exposed at ends.
3. Place a bacon slice on each strip, letting 0.3cm hang over. Season generously with pepper.
4. Roll pastry and bacon into pinwheels. Seal ends with water.
5. Preheat air fryer to 182°C/360°F.
6. Brush basket with oil. Add pinwheels and air fry 8 minutes. Flip and cook 2 more minutes.
7. Serve warm.

### Variations & Ingredients Tips:

- Use turkey or beef bacon instead.
- Sprinkle with grated parmesan before rolling.
- Dip in maple or ranch dressing for serving.

**Per Serving:** Calories: 230; Total Fat: 12g; Saturated Fat: 4g; Cholesterol: 15mg; Sodium: 410mg; Total Carbs: 24g; Dietary Fiber: 1g; Total Sugars: 8g; Protein: 6g

## Mascarpone Iced Cinnamon Rolls

**Servings: 6 | Prep Time: 20 Minutes | Cooking Time: 40 Minutes**

### Ingredients:

- 1/4 cup mascarpone cheese, softened
- 255g puff pastry sheet
- 3 tbsp light brown sugar
- 2 tsp ground cinnamon
- 2 tsp butter, melted
- 1/4 tsp vanilla extract
- 1/4 tsp salt
- 2 tbsp milk
- 1 tbsp lemon zest
- 1/4 cup confectioners' sugar

### Directions:

1. Preheat air fryer to 160°C/320°F.
2. Mix the brown sugar and cinnamon in a small bowl. Unroll the pastry sheet on its paper and brush it with melted butter. Then sprinkle with cinnamon sugar. Roll up the dough tightly, then cut into rolls about 5-cm wide. Put into a greased baking pan with the spiral side showing. Put the pan into the air fryer and Bake until golden brown, 18-20 minutes. Set aside to cool for 5-10 minutes.
3. Meanwhile, add the mascarpone cheese, vanilla, and salt in a small bowl, whisking until smooth and creamy. Add the confectioners' sugar and continue whisking until fully blended. Pour and mix in 1 tsp of milk at a time until the glaze is pourable but still with some thickness.
4. Spread the glaze over the warm cinnamon rolls and scatter with lemon zest. Serve and enjoy!

### Variations & Ingredients Tips:

- Use cream cheese or ricotta instead of mascarpone.
- Add some chopped pecans or walnuts to the filling.
- Serve with fresh berries or a scoop of vanilla ice cream.

**Per Serving:** Calories: 340; Total Fat: 22g; Saturated Fat: 9g; Cholesterol: 30mg; Sodium: 290mg; Total Carbs: 31g; Dietary Fiber: 1g; Total Sugars: 13g; Protein: 5g

## Apricot-cheese Mini Pies

**Servings: 6 | Prep Time: 20 Minutes | Cooking Time: 35 Minutes**

### Ingredients:

- 2 refrigerated pie crusts
- 1/3 cup apricot preserves
- 1 tsp cornstarch
- ½ cup vanilla yogurt
- 28g cream cheese
- 1 tsp sugar
- Rainbow sprinkles

### Directions:

1. Preheat air fryer to 188°C/370°F. Lay out pie crusts and cut each into three rectangles for 6 total.
2. Mix apricot preserves and cornstarch. Cover half of each rectangle with 1 tbsp preserve mixture.
3. Fold dough over and crimp edges with a fork to seal.
4. Lightly coat each pie with cooking oil and place in air fryer basket without stacking. Bake 10 minutes.
5. Meanwhile, mix yogurt, cream cheese and sugar for frosting.
6. Let pies cool completely, then frost and add sprinkles.

### Variations & Ingredients Tips:

- Use different fruit preserves like raspberry or strawberry

- Add spices like cinnamon to the frosting
- Brush pies with milk or egg wash before baking

**Per Serving:** Calories: 255; Total Fat: 13g; Saturated Fat: 4g; Cholesterol: 15mg; Sodium: 280mg; Total Carbs: 32g; Dietary Fiber: 1g; Total Sugars: 16g; Protein: 3g

## Lime Muffins

**Servings: 6 | Prep Time: 15 Minutes | Cooking Time: 30 Minutes**

### Ingredients:

- 1 ½ tbsp butter, softened
- 6 tbsp sugar
- 1 egg
- 1 egg white
- 1 tsp vanilla extract
- 1 tsp lime juice
- 1 lime, zested
- 150g Greek yogurt
- ¾ cup + 2 tbsp flour
- ¾ cup raspberries

### Directions:

1. Beat butter and sugar in a mixer for 2 minutes at medium speed. In a separate bowl, whisk together the egg, egg white and vanilla. Pour into the mixer bowl, add lime juice and zest. Beat until combined. At a low speed, add yogurt then flour.
2. Fold in the raspberries. Divide the mixture into 6 greased muffin cups using an ice cream scoop. The cups should be filled about ¾ of the way.
3. Preheat air fryer to 150°C/300°F. Put the muffins into the air fryer and Bake for 15 minutes until the tops are golden and a toothpick in the center comes out clean.
4. Allow to cool before serving.

### Variations & Ingredients Tips:

- Use lemon instead of lime for a different citrus flavor.
- Add some poppy seeds or shredded coconut to the batter.
- Top with a lime glaze made of powdered sugar and lime juice.

**Per Serving:** Calories: 200; Total Fat: 6g; Saturated Fat: 3g; Cholesterol: 40mg; Sodium: 55mg; Total Carbs: 32g; Dietary Fiber: 2g; Total Sugars: 19g; Protein: 6g

## Cinnamon Banana Bread With Pecans

**Servings: 6 | Prep Time: 10 Minutes | Cooking Time: 35 Minutes**

### Ingredients:

- 2 ripe bananas, mashed
- 1 egg
- ¼ cup Greek yogurt
- ¼ cup olive oil
- ½ teaspoon peppermint extract
- 2 tablespoons honey
- 1 cup flour
- ¼ teaspoon salt
- ¼ teaspoon baking soda
- ½ teaspoon ground cinnamon
- ¼ cup chopped pecans

### Directions:

1. Preheat air fryer to 180°C/360°F.
2. Add the bananas, egg, yogurt, olive oil, peppermint, and honey in a large bowl and mix until combined and mostly smooth.
3. Sift the flour, salt, baking soda, and cinnamon into the wet mixture, then stir until just combined.
4. Gently fold in the pecans. Spread to distribute evenly into a greased loaf pan.
5. Place the loaf pan in the frying basket and Bake for 23 minutes or until golden brown on top and a toothpick inserted into the center comes out clean.
6. Allow to cool for 5 minutes. Serve.

### Variations & Ingredients Tips:

- Use different types of mix-ins, such as chocolate chips or dried fruit, for a variety of flavors and textures.
- Add some grated carrots or zucchini to the batter for extra moisture and nutrients.
- For a vegan version, replace the egg with a flax egg and use non-dairy yogurt.

**Per Serving:** Calories: 270; Total Fat: 14g; Saturated Fat: 2g; Cholesterol: 30mg; Sodium: 180mg; Total Carbs: 34g; Fiber: 2g; Sugars: 14g; Protein: 4g

## Tri-color Frittata

**Servings: 4 | Prep Time: 10 Minutes | Cooking Time: 30 Minutes**

### Ingredients:

- 8 eggs, beaten
- 1 red bell pepper, diced
- Salt and pepper to taste
- 1 garlic clove, minced
- ½ tsp dried oregano
- ½ cup ricotta

### Directions:

1. Preheat air fryer to 180°C/360°F.
2. Place the beaten eggs, bell pepper, oregano, salt, black pepper, and garlic and mix well.
3. Fold in ¼ cup half of ricotta cheese.
4. Pour the egg mixture into a greased cake pan and top with the remaining ricotta.
5. Place into the air fryer and Bake for 18-20 minutes or until the eggs are set in the center.
6. Let the frittata cool for 5 minutes. Serve sliced.

### Variations & Ingredients Tips:

- Add spinach, tomatoes or mushrooms to the egg mixture.
- Use feta or goat cheese instead of ricotta.
- Top with avocado slices and salsa for serving.

**Per Serving:** Calories: 203; Total Fat: 14g; Saturated Fat: 6g;

Cholesterol: 387mg; Sodium: 243mg; Total Carbs: 4g; Dietary Fiber: 1g; Total Sugars: 3g; Protein: 15g

## Cheddar & Sausage Tater Tots

**Servings: 4 | Prep Time: 10 Minutes | Cooking Time: 25 Minutes**

### Ingredients:

- 340g ground chicken sausage
- 4 eggs
- 1 cup sour cream
- 1 tsp Worcestershire sauce
- 1 tsp shallot powder
- Salt and pepper to taste
- 454g frozen tater tots
- ¾ cup grated cheddar

### Directions:

1. Whisk eggs, sour cream, Worcestershire, shallot powder, salt and pepper in a bowl.
2. Brown sausage in a skillet 3-4 mins, breaking into pieces. Set aside.
3. Preheat air fryer to 165°C/330°F.
4. Lightly grease a baking pan. Layer tater tots in pan and air fry 6 mins, shaking pan.
5. Top tots with sausage and egg mixture. Air fry 6 more mins.
6. Sprinkle with cheddar and cook 2-3 more mins until melted.
7. Serve warm.

### Variations & Ingredients Tips:

- Use pork or turkey sausage instead of chicken.
- Add diced peppers, onions or jalapeños to the mix.
- Substitute Greek yogurt for the sour cream.

**Per Serving:** Calories: 575; Total Fat: 35g; Saturated Fat: 13g; Cholesterol: 245mg; Sodium: 960mg; Total Carbs: 42g; Dietary Fiber: 3g; Total Sugars: 2g; Protein: 24g

## Cheesy Egg Popovers

**Servings: 6 | Prep Time: 5 Minutes | Cooking Time: 30 Minutes**

### Ingredients:

- 5 eggs
- 1 tbsp milk
- 2 tbsp heavy cream
- Salt and pepper to taste
- ⅛ tsp ground nutmeg
- ¼ cup grated Swiss cheese

### Directions:

1. Preheat air fryer to 177°C/350°F.
2. Beat all ingredients in a bowl.
3. Divide between greased muffin cups and place in air fryer basket.
4. Bake for 9 minutes.
5. Let cool slightly before serving.

### Variations & Ingredients Tips:

- Use different cheeses like cheddar or parmesan.
- Add chopped herbs, crumbled bacon or ham.
- Serve with hollandaise or cheese sauce for dipping.

**Per Serving:** Calories: 100; Total Fat: 7g; Saturated Fat: 3g; Cholesterol: 185mg; Sodium: 105mg; Total Carbs: 1g; Dietary Fiber: 0g; Total Sugars: 1g; Protein: 7g

## Chia Seed Banana Bread

**Servings: 6 | Prep Time: 10 Minutes | Cooking Time: 35 Minutes**

### Ingredients:

- 2 bananas, mashed
- 2 tbsp sunflower oil
- 2 tbsp maple syrup
- ½ tsp vanilla extract
- ½ tbsp chia seeds
- ½ tbsp ground flaxseeds
- 1 cup pastry flour
- ¼ cup sugar
- ½ tsp ground cinnamon
- 1 orange, zested
- ¼ tsp salt
- ¼ tsp ground nutmeg
- ½ tsp baking powder

### Directions:

1. Preheat air fryer to 177°C/350°F.
2. In a bowl, mix bananas, oil, syrup, vanilla, chia and flax seeds.
3. Add flour, sugar, cinnamon, orange zest, salt, nutmeg and baking powder. Stir to combine.
4. Pour batter into a greased baking pan and smooth top.
5. Bake for 25 minutes until a knife inserted in center comes out clean.
6. Remove, let cool briefly, then cut into wedges.
7. Serve warm.

### Variations & Ingredients Tips:

- Add chopped nuts or chocolate chips to the batter.
- Substitute whole wheat pastry flour for all-purpose.
- Top with streusel topping before baking.

**Per Serving:** Calories: 205; Total Fat: 6g; Saturated Fat: 0.5g; Cholesterol: 0mg; Sodium: 170mg; Total Carbs: 36g; Dietary Fiber: 4g; Total Sugars: 15g; Protein: 3g

## Mushroom & Cavolo Nero Egg Muffins

**Servings: 6 | Prep Time: 10 Minutes | Cooking Time: 20 Minutes**

### Ingredients:

- 225g baby Bella mushrooms, sliced

- 6 eggs, beaten
- 1 garlic clove, minced
- Salt and pepper to taste
- 1/2 tsp chili powder
- 1 cup cavolo nero (Tuscan kale), shredded
- 2 scallions, diced

### Directions:

1. Preheat air fryer to 160°C/320°F.
2. Place eggs, garlic, salt, pepper and chili powder in a bowl and beat well combined.
3. Fold in mushrooms, cavolo nero and scallions.
4. Divide mixture between greased muffin cups and place in air fryer basket.
5. Bake for 12-15 minutes until eggs are set.
6. Cool 5 minutes before serving.

### Variations & Ingredients Tips:

- Use different greens like spinach or chard.
- Add diced ham, bacon or cheese.
- Cook in oven-safe ramekins if air fryer cups are too small.

**Per Serving:** Calories: 75; Total Fat: 4g; Saturated Fat: 1g; Cholesterol: 155mg; Sodium: 90mg; Total Carbs: 4g; Dietary Fiber: 1g; Sugars: 2g; Protein: 6g

## Chili Hash Browns

**Servings: 4 | Prep Time: 10 Minutes | Cooking Time: 45 Minutes**

### Ingredients:

- 1 tablespoon ancho chili powder
- 1 tablespoon chipotle powder
- 2 teaspoons ground cumin
- 2 teaspoons smoked paprika
- 1 teaspoon garlic powder
- 1 teaspoon cayenne pepper
- Salt and pepper to taste
- 2 peeled russet potatoes, grated
- 2 tablespoons olive oil
- ⅓ cup chopped onion
- 3 garlic cloves, minced

### Directions:

1. Preheat the air fryer to 200°C/400°F.
2. Combine chili powder, cumin, paprika, garlic powder, chipotle, cayenne, and black pepper in a small bowl, then pour into a glass jar with a lid and store in a cool, dry place.
3. Add the olive oil, onion, and garlic to a cake pan, put it in the air fryer, and Bake for 3 minutes.
4. Put the grated potatoes in a bowl and sprinkle with 2 teaspoons of the spice mixture, toss and add them to the cake pan along with the onion mix.
5. Bake for 20-23 minutes, stirring once or until the potatoes are crispy and golden. Season with salt and serve.

### Variations & Ingredients Tips:

- Use different types of potatoes, such as sweet potatoes or Yukon Gold, for a variety of flavors and textures.
- Add some diced bell peppers or jalapeños to the hash browns for extra vegetables and heat.
- Serve the hash browns with a side of salsa or sour cream for a Mexican-inspired breakfast.

**Per Serving:** Calories: 220; Total Fat: 7g; Saturated Fat: 1g; Cholesterol: 0mg; Sodium: 50mg; Total Carbs: 36g; Fiber: 4g; Sugars: 2g; Protein: 5g

## Egg And Sausage Crescent Rolls

**Servings: 8 | Prep Time: 15 Minutes | Cooking Time: 11 Minutes**

### Ingredients:

- 5 large eggs
- ¼ teaspoon black pepper
- ¼ teaspoon salt
- 1 tablespoon milk
- ¼ cup shredded cheddar cheese
- One 226 g package refrigerated crescent rolls
- 60 g pesto sauce
- 8 fully cooked breakfast sausage links, defrosted

### Directions:

1. Preheat the air fryer to 160°C/320°F.
2. In a medium bowl, crack the eggs and whisk with the pepper, salt, and milk. Pour into a frying pan over medium heat and scramble. Just before the eggs are done, turn off the heat and add in the cheese. Continue to cook until the cheese has melted and the eggs are finished (about 5 minutes total). Remove from the heat.
3. Remove the crescent rolls from the package and press them flat onto a clean surface lightly dusted with flour. Add 1½ teaspoons of pesto sauce across the center of each roll. Place equal portions of eggs across all 8 rolls. Then top each roll with a sausage link and roll the dough up tight so it resembles the crescent-roll shape.
4. Lightly spray your air fryer basket with olive oil mist and place the rolls on top. Bake for 6 minutes or until the tops of the rolls are lightly browned.
5. Remove and let cool 3 to 5 minutes before serving.

### Variations & Ingredients Tips:

- Use turkey sausage or vegetarian sausage patties for a healthier twist.
- Add some sautéed spinach or kale to the egg mixture for extra greens.
- Brush the rolls with garlic butter before air frying for extra flavor.

**Per Serving:** Calories: 258; Total Fat: 18g; Saturated Fat: 6g; Cholesterol: 153mg; Sodium: 515mg; Total Carbs: 13g; Dietary Fiber: 0g; Total Sugars: 4g; Protein: 11g

## Herby Parmesan Pita

**Servings: 2 | Prep Time: 5 Minutes | Cooking Time: 15 Minutes**

### Ingredients:

- 1 whole-wheat pita
- 2 teaspoons olive oil
- ¼ sweet onion, diced
- ¼ teaspoon garlic, minced
- 1 egg
- ¼ teaspoon dried tarragon
- ¼ teaspoon dried thyme
- ⅛ teaspoon salt
- 3 teaspoons grated Parmesan cheese

### Directions:

1. Preheat air fryer to 190°C/380°F. Lightly brush the top of the pita with olive oil, then top with onion and garlic. Crack the egg into a small bowl and sprinkle it with tarragon, thyme, and salt. Place the pita in the frying basket and gently pour the egg onto the top of the pita. Sprinkle with cheese over the top. Bake for 6 minutes. Leave to cool for 5 minutes. Cut into pieces and serve.

### Variations & Ingredients Tips:

- Use naan, flatbread or tortilla instead of pita for a different base.
- Add some chopped spinach, tomatoes or bell peppers on top for extra veggies.
- Swap Parmesan for feta, goat cheese or mozzarella for different flavors.

**Per Serving:** Calories: 172; Total Fat: 9g; Saturated Fat: 2g; Cholesterol: 96mg; Sodium: 368mg; Total Carbs: 17g; Dietary Fiber: 3g; Total Sugars: 2g; Protein: 8g

## Oat & Nut Granola

**Servings: 6 | Prep Time: 10 Minutes | Cooking Time: 25 Minutes**

### Ingredients:

- 2 cups rolled oats
- ¼ cup pistachios
- ¼ cup chopped almonds
- ¼ cup chopped cashews
- ¼ cup honey
- 2 tbsp light brown sugar
- 3 tbsp butter
- ½ tsp ground cinnamon
- ½ cup dried figs

### Directions:

1. Preheat the air fryer to 165°C/325°F.
2. Combine the oats, pistachios, almonds, and cashews in a bowl and toss, then set aside.
3. In a saucepan, cook the honey, brown sugar, butter, and cinnamon over low heat, stirring frequently, for 4 minutes. Melt the butter completely and make sure the mixture is smooth.
4. Pour over the oat mix and stir.
5. Scoop the granola mixture into a greased baking pan. Put the pan in the frying basket and bake for 7 minutes.
6. Remove the pan and stir. Cook for another 6-9 minutes or until the granola is golden.
7. Add the dried figs and stir. Remove the pan and let cool.
8. Store in a covered container at room temperature for up to 3 days.

### Variations & Ingredients Tips:

- Use different nuts or seeds.
- Drizzle with melted chocolate after baking.
- Add coconut flakes or dried fruit.

**Per Serving:** Calories: 349; Total Fat: 15.8g; Saturated Fat: 4.2g; Cholesterol: 13mg; Sodium: 46mg; Total Carbohydrates: 48.3g; Dietary Fiber: 5.9g; Total Sugars: 21.2g; Protein: 7.2g

## Mediterranean Granola

**Servings: 6 | Prep Time: 10 Minutes | Cooking Time: 40 Minutes**

### Ingredients:

- 1 cup rolled oats
- 1/4 cup dried cherries, diced
- 1/4 cup almond slivers
- 1/4 cup hazelnuts, chopped
- 1/4 cup pepitas
- 1/4 cup hemp hearts
- 3 tbsp honey
- 1 tbsp olive oil
- 1 tsp ground cinnamon
- 1/4 tsp ground nutmeg
- 1/4 tsp salt
- 2 tbsp dark chocolate chips
- 3 cups Greek yogurt

### Directions:

1. Preheat air fryer to 130°C/260°F.
2. Stir the oats, cherries, almonds, hazelnuts, pepitas, hemp hearts, 2 tbsp of honey, olive oil, cinnamon, nutmeg, and salt in a bowl, mixing well.
3. Pour the mixture onto the parchment-lined frying basket and spread it into a single layer. Bake for 25-30 minutes, shaking twice.
4. Let the granola cool completely. Stir in the chocolate chips.
5. Divide between 6 cups. Top with Greek yogurt and remaining honey to serve.

### Variations & Ingredients Tips:

- Use dried apricots, figs or dates instead of cherries.
- Add some chia seeds or flax meal for extra nutrition.
- Serve with milk, almond milk or coconut yogurt.

**Per Serving:** Calories: 370; Total Fat: 18g; Saturated Fat: 4g; Cholesterol: 5mg; Sodium: 105mg; Total Carbs: 43g; Dietary Fiber: 6g; Total Sugars: 21g; Protein: 15g

## Cinnamon Biscuit Rolls

**Servings: 12 | Prep Time: 45 Minutes | Cooking Time: 5 Minutes**

### Ingredients:

- Dough
- ¼ cup warm water (40-46°C)
- 1 teaspoon active dry yeast
- 1 tablespoon sugar
- ½ cup buttermilk, lukewarm
- 2 cups flour, plus more for dusting
- 1 teaspoon baking powder
- ½ teaspoon salt
- 3 tablespoons cold butter
- Filling
- 1 tablespoon butter, melted
- 1 teaspoon cinnamon
- 2 tablespoons sugar
- Icing
- ⅔ cup powdered sugar
- ¼ teaspoon vanilla
- 2–3 teaspoons milk

### Directions:

1. Dissolve yeast and sugar in warm water. Add buttermilk, stir, and set aside.
2. In a large bowl, sift together flour, baking powder, and salt. Using knives or a pastry blender, cut in butter until mixture is well combined and crumbly.
3. Pour in buttermilk mixture and stir with fork until a ball of dough forms.
4. Knead dough on a lightly floured surface for 5 minutes. Roll into a 20 x 28 cm rectangle.
5. For the filling, spread the melted butter over the dough.
6. In a small bowl, stir together the cinnamon and sugar, then sprinkle over dough.
7. Starting on a long side, roll up dough so that you have a roll about 28 cm long. Cut into 12 slices with a serrated knife and sawing motion so slices remain round.
8. Place rolls on a plate or cookie sheet about 2.5 cm apart and let rise for 30 minutes.
9. For icing, mix the powdered sugar, vanilla, and milk. Stir and add additional milk until icing reaches a good spreading consistency.
10. Preheat air fryer to 180°C/360°F.
11. Place 6 cinnamon rolls in basket and cook 5 minutes or until top springs back when lightly touched. Repeat to cook remaining 6 rolls.
12. Spread icing over warm rolls and serve.

### Variations & Ingredients Tips:

- Use different types of filling, such as cream cheese or fruit jam, for a variety of flavors.
- Add some chopped nuts or raisins to the filling for extra texture.
- For a savory version, replace the cinnamon and sugar with garlic powder and herbs, and skip the icing.

**Per Serving:** Calories: 210; Total Fat: 6g; Saturated Fat: 3.5g; Cholesterol: 15mg; Sodium: 200mg; Total Carbs: 36g; Fiber: 1g; Sugars: 14g; Protein: 4g

## Morning Loaded Potato Skins

**Servings: 4 | Prep Time: 15 Minutes | Cooking Time: 55 Minutes**

### Ingredients:

- 2 large potatoes
- 1 fried bacon slice, chopped
- Salt and pepper to taste
- 1 tbsp chopped dill
- 1 1/2 tbsp butter
- 2 tbsp milk
- 4 eggs
- 1 scallion, sliced
- 1/4 cup grated fontina cheese
- 2 tbsp chopped parsley

### Directions:

1. Preheat air fryer to 200°C/400°F. Poke holes in potatoes and bake 40-45 mins until soft.
2. Cut potatoes in half lengthwise. Scoop out flesh, leaving 1.3-cm shell.
3. Mash flesh with bacon, salt, pepper, dill, butter and milk.
4. Fill potato skins with mashed potato. Make a 1.3cm deep indent in the center.
5. Crack an egg into each indentation. Top with scallions and cheese.
6. Air fry 3-5 more mins until egg is cooked and cheese melts.
7. Garnish with parsley before serving.

### Variations & Ingredients Tips:

- Add cooked chorizo, ham or sauteed spinach to the filling.
- Bake potatoes in the oven first if your air fryer is too small.
- Use cheddar or pepper jack cheese instead of fontina.

**Per Serving:** Calories: 300; Total Fat: 15g; Saturated Fat: 8g; Cholesterol: 215mg; Sodium: 290mg; Total Carbs: 30g; Dietary Fiber: 3g; Sugars: 2g; Protein: 12g

## Colorful French Toast Sticks

**Servings: 4 | Prep Time: 10 Minutes | Cooking Time: 20 Minutes**

### Ingredients:

- 1 egg
- ⅓ cup whole milk
- Salt to taste
- ½ teaspoon ground cinnamon
- ½ teaspoon ground chia seeds
- 1 cup crushed pebbles
- 4 sandwich bread slices, each cut into 4 sticks
- ¼ cup honey

### Directions:

1. Preheat air fryer at 190°C/375°F.
2. Whisk the egg, milk, salt, cinnamon and chia seeds in a bowl. In another bowl, add crushed cereal.

3. Dip breadsticks in the egg mixture, then dredge them in the cereal crumbs.
4. Place breadsticks in the greased frying basket and Air Fry for 5 minutes, flipping once.
5. Serve with honey as a dip.

### Variations & Ingredients Tips:

- Use different types of bread, such as whole wheat or brioche, for a variety of flavors and textures.
- Add some vanilla extract or orange zest to the egg mixture for extra flavor.
- For a savory version, replace the cinnamon and honey with garlic powder and marinara sauce for dipping.

**Per Serving:** Calories: 240; Total Fat: 5g; Saturated Fat: 1.5g; Cholesterol: 50mg; Sodium: 330mg; Total Carbs: 43g; Fiber: 2g; Sugars: 18g; Protein: 7g

## Honey Donuts

**Servings: 6 | Prep Time: 20 Minutes | Cooking Time: 25 Minutes + Chilling Time**

### Ingredients:

- 1 refrigerated puff pastry sheet
- 2 teaspoons flour
- 155 g powdered sugar
- 3 tablespoons honey
- 2 tablespoons milk
- 2 tablespoons butter, melted
- ½ teaspoon vanilla extract
- ½ teaspoon ground cinnamon
- Pinch of salt

### Directions:

1. Preheat the air fryer to 165°C/325°F. Dust a clean work surface with flour and lay the puff pastry on it, then cut crosswise into five 7.5 cm wide strips. Cut each strip into thirds for 15 squares. Lay round parchment paper in the bottom of the basket, then add the pastry squares in a single layer.
2. Make sure none are touching. Bake for 13-18 minutes or until brown, then leave on a rack to cool. Repeat for all dough. Combine the sugar, honey, milk, butter, vanilla, cinnamon, and salt in a small bowl and mix with a wire whisk until combined. Dip the top half of each donut in the glaze, turn the donut glaze side up, and return to the wire rack. Let cool until the glaze sets, then serve.

### Variations & Ingredients Tips:

- Fill the donuts with pastry cream, jam or Nutella before glazing.
- Sprinkle the glaze with chopped nuts, sprinkles or shredded coconut.
- Flavor the glaze with lemon zest, orange zest or maple extract for variety.

**Per Serving:** Calories: 394; Total Fat: 19g; Saturated Fat: 6g; Cholesterol: 10mg; Sodium: 190mg; Total Carbs: 54g; Dietary Fiber: 1g; Total Sugars: 35g; Protein: 4g

## Thai Turkey Sausage Patties

**Servings: 4 | Prep Time: 10 Minutes | Cooking Time: 30 Minutes**

### Ingredients:

- 340g turkey sausage
- 1 tsp onion powder
- 1 tsp dried coriander
- ¼ tsp Thai curry paste
- ¼ tsp red pepper flakes
- Salt and pepper to taste

### Directions:

1. Preheat air fryer to 175°C/350°F.
2. Place the sausage, onion powder, coriander, curry paste, red pepper flakes, salt, and black pepper in a large bowl and mix well.
3. Form into eight patties.
4. Arrange the patties on the greased air fryer basket and air fry for 10 minutes, flipping once halfway through.
5. Once cooked, transfer patties to a plate and serve hot.

### Variations & Ingredients Tips:

- Use ground turkey or chicken instead of sausage.
- Add grated ginger or lemongrass for more Thai flavor.
- Serve with a sweet chili sauce for dipping.

**Per Serving:** Calories: 195; Total Fat: 12g; Saturated Fat: 3g; Cholesterol: 70mg; Sodium: 540mg; Total Carbs: 2g; Dietary Fiber: 1g; Total Sugars: 0g; Protein: 20g

# Fish And Seafood Recipes

### Coconut-shrimp Po' Boys

**Servings: 4 | Prep Time: 15 Minutes | Cooking Time: 5 Minutes**

Ingredients:

- 1/2 cup cornstarch
- 2 eggs
- 2 tablespoons milk
- 3/4 cup shredded coconut
- 1/2 cup panko breadcrumbs
- 450g (31-35 count) shrimp, peeled and deveined
- Old Bay Seasoning
- Oil for misting or cooking spray
- 2 large hoagie rolls
- Honey mustard or light mayonnaise
- 1 1/2 cups shredded lettuce
- 1 large tomato, thinly sliced

Directions:

1. Place cornstarch in a shallow dish.
2. In another dish, beat eggs and milk.
3. In a third dish mix coconut and panko crumbs.
4. Season shrimp with Old Bay.
5. Dip shrimp in cornstarch, egg, then coconut mixture.
6. Mist shrimp with oil on both sides.
7. Air fry half the shrimp for 5 mins at 200°C/390°F.
8. Repeat for remaining shrimp.
9. To Assemble:
10. 1. Split hoagies, leaving one edge intact.
11. 2. Air fry 1-2 mins until heated.
12. 3. Spread with honey mustard/mayo.
13. 4. Top with lettuce, tomato and shrimp.

Variations & Ingredients Tips:

- Use cajun seasoning or garlic powder instead of Old Bay.
- Add sliced pickles or remoulade sauce.
- Serve on regular sandwich rolls instead of hoagies.

**Per Serving:** Calories: 389; Total Fat: 10g; Saturated Fat: 3g; Cholesterol: 225mg; Sodium: 662mg; Total Carbs: 45g; Dietary Fiber: 3g; Total Sugars: 5g; Protein: 29g

### Cajun-seasoned Shrimp

**Servings: 2 | Prep Time: 5 Minutes | Cooking Time: 15 Minutes**

Ingredients:

- 454 grams shelled tail on shrimp, deveined
- 2 tsp grated Parmesan cheese
- 2 tbsp butter, melted
- 1 tsp cayenne pepper
- 1 tsp garlic powder
- 2 tsp Cajun seasoning
- 1 tbsp lemon juice

Directions:

1. Preheat air fryer at 180°C/350°F.
2. Toss the shrimp, melted butter, cayenne pepper, garlic powder and cajun seasoning in a bowl, place them in the greased air fryer basket, and Air Fry for 6 minutes, flipping once.
3. Transfer it to a plate. Squeeze lemon juice over shrimp and stir in Parmesan cheese.
4. Serve immediately.

Variations & Ingredients Tips:

- Use peeled, deveined shrimp with or without tails for easier eating.
- Add a dash of hot sauce or red pepper flakes for extra heat.
- Serve over rice, pasta, or in tacos or po' boy sandwiches.

**Per Serving:** Calories: 400; Total Fat: 22g; Saturated Fat: 12g; Sodium: 2040mg; Total Carbohydrates: 4g; Dietary Fiber: 1g; Total Sugars: 0g; Protein: 45g

### Super Crunchy Flounder Fillets

**Servings: 2 | Prep Time: 10 Minutes | Cooking Time: 6 Minutes**

Ingredients:

- ½ cup all-purpose flour or tapioca flour
- 1 large egg white
- 1 tbsp water
- ¾ tsp table salt
- 1 cup plain panko bread crumbs (gluten-free, if a concern)
- 2 112g skinless flounder fillets
- Vegetable oil spray

Directions:

1. Preheat the air fryer to 200°C/400°F.
2. Set up and fill three shallow soup plates or small pie plates on your counter: one for the flour; one for the egg white, beaten with the water and salt until foamy; and one for the bread crumbs.
3. Dip one fillet in the flour, turning it to coat both sides. Gently shake off any excess flour, then dip the fillet in the egg white mixture, turning it to coat. Let any excess egg white mixture slip back into the rest, then set the fish in the bread crumbs. Turn it several times, gently pressing it into the crumbs to create an even crust. Generously coat both sides of the fillet with vegetable oil spray. If necessary, set it

aside and continue coating the remaining fillet in the same way.
4. Set the fillets in the basket. If working with more than one fillet, they should not touch, although they may be quite close together, depending on the basket's size. Air-fry undisturbed for 6 minutes, or until lightly browned and crunchy.
5. Use a nonstick-safe spatula to transfer the fillets to a wire rack. Cool for only a minute or two before serving.

### Variations & Ingredients Tips:

- Use cod, sole, or tilapia instead of flounder.
- Mix some grated Parmesan into the breadcrumbs for cheesy flavor.
- Serve with lemon wedges and tartar sauce on the side.

**Per Serving:** Calories: 270; Total Fat: 3g; Saturated Fat: 0.5g; Cholesterol: 75mg; Sodium: 900mg; Total Carbohydrates: 33g; Dietary Fiber: 1g; Total Sugars: 2g; Protein: 26g

## Crispy Sweet-and-sour Cod Fillets

**Servings: 3 | Prep Time: 10 Minutes | Cooking Time: 12 Minutes**

### Ingredients:

- 1 1/2 cups plain panko bread crumbs (gluten-free, if a concern)
- 2 tablespoons regular or low-fat mayonnaise (not fat-free; gluten-free, if a concern)
- 1/4 cup sweet pickle relish
- 3 (115to 140g) skinless cod fillets

### Directions:

1. Preheat the air fryer to 200°C/400°F.
2. Pour the bread crumbs into a shallow soup plate or a small pie plate.
3. Mix the mayonnaise and relish in a small bowl until well combined. Smear this mixture all over the cod fillets. Set them in the crumbs and turn until evenly coated on all sides, even on the ends.
4. Set the coated cod fillets in the basket with as much air space between them as possible. They should not touch. Air-fry undisturbed for 12 minutes, or until browned and crisp.
5. Use a nonstick-safe spatula to transfer the cod pieces to a wire rack. Cool for only a minute or two before serving hot.

### Variations & Ingredients Tips:

- Use tilapia, basa or catfish instead of cod.
- Substitute pickle relish with sweet chili sauce or mango chutney.
- Sprinkle with chopped scallions and toasted sesame seeds before serving.

**Per Serving:** Calories: 280; Total Fat: 8g; Saturated Fat: 1.5g; Cholesterol: 85mg; Sodium: 630mg; Total Carbs: 24g; Dietary Fiber: 1g; Total Sugars: 5g; Protein: 27g

## Lime Halibut Parcels

**Servings: 4 | Prep Time: 15 Minutes | Cooking Time: 45 Minutes**

### Ingredients:

- 1 lime, sliced
- 4 halibut fillets
- 1 tsp dried thyme
- Salt and pepper to taste
- 1 shredded carrot
- 1 red bell pepper, sliced
- 1/2 cup sliced celery
- 2 tbsp butter

### Directions:

1. Preheat air fryer to 200°C/400°F.
2. Make 4 parchment paper parcels place lime slices, halibut fillet, thyme, salt, pepper, veggies and butter in center.
3. Crimp and seal parcels tightly.
4. Place 2 parcels in air fryer basket on a rack, seam-side up.
5. Bake for 12-14 mins until puffed up and fish flakes.
6. Repeat with remaining 2 parcels. Caution: hot steam when opened.

### Variations & Ingredients Tips:

- Use other firm white fish like cod or snapper.
- Add lemon slices or white wine to the parcels.
- Serve over rice or with roasted potatoes.

**Per Serving:** Calories: 230; Total Fat: 8g; Saturated Fat: 4g; Cholesterol: 78mg; Sodium: 293mg; Total Carbs: 9g; Dietary Fiber: 2g; Total Sugars: 3g; Protein: 29g

## Saucy Shrimp

**Servings: 4 | Prep Time: 15 Minutes | Cooking Time: 30 Minutes**

### Ingredients:

- 450g peeled shrimp, deveined
- 1/2 cup grated coconut
- 1/4 cup bread crumbs
- 1/4 cup flour
- 1/4 tsp smoked paprika
- Salt and pepper to taste
- 1 egg
- 2 tbsp maple syrup
- 1/2 tsp rice vinegar
- 1 tbsp hot sauce
- 1/8 tsp red pepper flakes
- 1/4 cup orange juice
- 1 tsp cornstarch
- 1/2 cup banana ketchup
- 1 lemon, sliced

### Directions:

1. Preheat air fryer to 175°C/350°F.
2. Combine coconut, crumbs, flour, paprika, salt & pepper in a bowl.
3. In another bowl, whisk egg with 1 tsp water.

4. Dip shrimp in egg, then coat in crumb mixture.
5. Arrange shrimp in greased frying basket. Air Fry 5 mins, flip and cook 2-3 more mins.
6. Make sauce: In a pan, add syrup, ketchup, hot sauce, vinegar, pepper flakes. Make slurry with OJ and cornstarch.
7. Add slurry to pan, boil 5 mins until thick. Let sit 5 mins.
8. Serve shrimp with sauce and lemon wedges.

### Variations & Ingredients Tips:

- Substitute honey or agave for maple syrup.
- Add chopped pineapple or mango to the sauce.
- Toss cooked shrimp in the sauce instead of serving on the side.

**Per Serving:** Calories: 290; Total Fat: 7g; Saturated Fat: 4g; Cholesterol: 170mg; Sodium: 1050mg; Total Carbs: 37g; Dietary Fiber: 2g; Sugars: 17g; Protein: 20g

## Shrimp Al Pesto

**Servings: 4 | Prep Time: 5 Minutes | Cooking Time: 10 Minutes**

### Ingredients:

- 450g peeled shrimp, deveined
- 1/4 cup pesto sauce
- 1 lime, sliced
- 2 cups cooked farro

### Directions:

1. Preheat air fryer to 180°C/360°F.
2. Coat the shrimp with the pesto sauce in a bowl.
3. Put the shrimp in a single layer in the frying basket. Place the lime slices over the shrimp.
4. Roast for 5 minutes. Remove lime and discard.
5. Serve the shrimp over a bed of farro pilaf. Enjoy!

### Variations & Ingredients Tips:

- Use your favorite store-bought or homemade pesto.
- Add cherry tomatoes or sliced zucchini to the basket.
- Swap farro for rice, quinoa or pasta.

**Per Serving:** Calories: 250; Total Fat: 9g; Saturated Fat: 2g; Cholesterol: 170mg; Sodium: 480mg; Total Carbs: 21g; Dietary Fiber: 3g; Sugars: 2g; Protein: 21g

## Spicy Fish Street Tacos With Sriracha Slaw

**Servings: 2 | Prep Time: 10 Minutes | Cooking Time: 5 Minutes**

### Ingredients:

- Sriracha Slaw:
- 1/2 cup mayonnaise
- 2 tablespoons rice vinegar
- 1 teaspoon sugar
- 2 tablespoons sriracha chili sauce
- 5 cups shredded green cabbage
- 1/4 cup shredded carrots
- 2 scallions, chopped
- Salt and freshly ground black pepper
- Tacos:
- 1/2 cup flour
- 1 teaspoon chili powder
- 1/2 teaspoon ground cumin
- 1 teaspoon salt
- Freshly ground black pepper
- 1/2 teaspoon baking powder
- 1 egg, beaten
- 1/4 cup milk
- 1 cup breadcrumbs
- 450g mahi-mahi or snapper fillets
- 1 tablespoon canola or vegetable oil
- 6 (15cm) flour tortillas
- 1 lime, cut into wedges

### Directions:

1. Make sriracha slaw by combining mayo, vinegar, sugar, sriracha in a bowl. Add cabbage, carrots, scallions and season. Refrigerate.
2. In a bowl, mix flour, chili, cumin, salt, pepper and baking powder. Add egg and milk to make a batter.
3. Cut fish into 2.5cm x 10cm strips. Dip in batter, then coat in breadcrumbs.
4. Preheat air fryer to 200°C/400°F. Spray fish with oil.
5. Air fry fish 3 mins, flip and fry 2 more mins until crispy.
6. Warm tortillas. Assemble tacos with fish, slaw and lime wedges.

### Variations & Ingredients Tips:

- Use cod, tilapia or other white fish.
- Add shredded purple cabbage to the slaw.
- Serve with avocado, pico de gallo or sour cream.

**Per Serving:** Calories: 670; Total Fat: 26g; Saturated Fat: 4g; Cholesterol: 165mg; Sodium: 1590mg; Total Carbs: 77g; Dietary Fiber: 7g; Sugars: 11g; Protein: 35g

## Basil Crab Cakes With Fresh Salad

**Servings: 2 | Prep Time: 15 Minutes | Cooking Time: 25 Minutes**

### Ingredients:

- 225g lump crabmeat
- 2 tbsp mayonnaise
- 1/2 tsp Dijon mustard
- 1/2 tsp lemon juice
- 1/2 tsp lemon zest
- 2 tsp minced yellow onion
- 1/4 tsp prepared horseradish
- 1/4 cup flour
- 1 egg white, beaten
- 1 tbsp basil, minced
- 1 tbsp olive oil
- 2 tsp white wine vinegar
- Salt and pepper to taste
- 115g arugula
- 1/2 cup blackberries
- 1/4 cup pine nuts
- 2 lemon wedges

### Directions:

1. Preheat air fryer to 200°C/400°F.

2. Combine the crabmeat, mayonnaise, mustard, lemon juice and zest, onion, horseradish, flour, egg white, and basil in a bowl. Form mixture into 4 patties.
3. Place the patties in the lightly greased frying basket and Air Fry for 10 minutes, flipping once.
4. Combine olive oil, vinegar, salt, and pepper in a bowl. Toss in the arugula and share into 2 medium bowls. Add 2 crab cakes to each bowl and scatter with blackberries, pine nuts, and lemon wedges.
5. Serve warm.

### Variations & Ingredients Tips:

- Add some diced red bell pepper or celery to the crab cake mixture.
- Use mixed greens or baby spinach instead of arugula.
- Serve with a remoulade or spicy mayo sauce.

**Per Serving:** Calories: 440; Total Fat: 29g; Saturated Fat: 4g; Cholesterol: 115mg; Sodium: 830mg; Total Carbs: 19g; Dietary Fiber: 4g; Total Sugars: 6g; Protein: 30g

## Fish And "chips"

**Servings: 2 | Prep Time: 15 Minutes | Cooking Time: 10 Minutes**

### Ingredients:

- 1/2 cup flour
- 1/2 teaspoon paprika
- 1/4 teaspoon ground white pepper (or freshly ground black pepper)
- 1 egg
- 1/4 cup mayonnaise
- 2 cups salt & vinegar kettle cooked potato chips, coarsely crushed
- 340g cod
- Tartar sauce
- Lemon wedges

### Directions:

1. Set up a dredging station. Combine the flour, paprika and pepper in a shallow dish. Combine the egg and mayonnaise in a second shallow dish. Place the crushed potato chips in a third shallow dish.
2. Cut the cod into 6 pieces. Dredge each piece of fish in the flour, then dip it into the egg mixture and then place it into the crushed potato chips. Make sure all sides of the fish are covered and pat the chips gently onto the fish so they stick well.
3. Preheat the air fryer to 190°C/370°F.
4. Place the coated fish fillets into the air fry basket. (It is ok if a couple of pieces slightly overlap or rest on top of other fillets in order to fit everything in the basket.)
5. Air-fry for 10 minutes, gently turning the fish over halfway through the cooking time.
6. Transfer the fish to a platter and serve with tartar sauce and lemon wedges.

### Variations & Ingredients Tips:

- Use haddock, pollack or catfish instead of cod.
- Substitute potato chips with panko breadcrumbs or crushed cornflakes.
- Serve with malt vinegar, coleslaw and mushy peas.

**Per Serving:** Calories: 520; Total Fat: 27g; Saturated Fat: 5g; Cholesterol: 155mg; Sodium: 570mg; Total Carbs: 35g; Dietary Fiber: 1g; Total Sugars: 1g; Protein: 35g

## Speedy Shrimp Paella

**Servings: 4 | Prep Time: 10 Minutes | Cooking Time: 20 Minutes**

### Ingredients:

- 2 cups cooked rice
- 1 red bell pepper, chopped
- 1/4 cup vegetable broth
- 1/2 tsp turmeric
- 1/2 tsp dried thyme
- 1 cup cooked small shrimp
- 1/2 cup baby peas
- 1 tomato, diced

### Directions:

1. Preheat air fryer to 170°C/340°F.
2. Gently combine rice, bell pepper, broth, turmeric and thyme in a baking pan.
3. Bake in air fryer until rice is hot, about 9 minutes.
4. Remove pan, stir in shrimp, peas and tomato.
5. Return to air fryer and cook until bubbling and hot, 5-8 more minutes.
6. Serve and enjoy!

### Variations & Ingredients Tips:

- Use chicken or vegetable broth for more flavor.
- Add sliced chorizo or bacon for a smoky flavor.
- Stir in lemon juice or chopped parsley before serving.

**Per Serving:** Calories: 180; Total Fat: 2g; Saturated Fat: 0g; Cholesterol: 35mg; Sodium: 120mg; Total Carbs: 32g; Dietary Fiber: 3g; Sugars: 4g; Protein: 9g

## French Grouper Nicoise

**Servings: 4 | Prep Time: 10 Minutes | Cooking Time: 20 Minutes**

### Ingredients:

- 4 grouper fillets
- Salt to taste
- 1/2 tsp ground cumin
- 3 garlic cloves, minced
- 1 tomato, sliced
- 1/4 cup sliced Nicoise olives
- 1/4 cup dill, chopped
- 1 lemon, juiced
- 1/4 cup olive oil

### Directions:

1. Preheat air fryer to 195°C/380°F.
2. Season grouper fillets with salt and cumin.

3. Arrange fillets in greased air fryer basket.
4. Top with garlic, tomato, olives and fresh dill.
5. Drizzle with lemon juice and olive oil.
6. Bake for 10-12 minutes.
7. Serve and enjoy!

### Variations & Ingredients Tips:

- Use other white fish like halibut or cod.
- Add capers, red onion or roasted red peppers.
- Serve over arugula or with roasted potatoes.

**Per Serving:** Calories: 275; Total Fat: 13g; Saturated Fat: 2g; Cholesterol: 86mg; Sodium: 267mg; Total Carbs: 3g; Dietary Fiber: 1g; Total Sugars: 0g; Protein: 35g

## Nutty Shrimp With Amaretto Glaze

**Servings: 10 | Prep Time: 10 Minutes | Cooking Time: 10 Minutes**

### Ingredients:

- 1 cup flour
- 1/2 teaspoon baking powder
- 1 teaspoon salt
- 2 eggs, beaten
- 1/2 cup milk
- 2 tablespoons olive or vegetable oil
- 2 cups sliced almonds
- 900g large shrimp, peeled and deveined, tails left on
- 2 cups amaretto liqueur

### Directions:

1. Combine the flour, baking powder and salt in a large bowl. Add the eggs, milk and oil and stir until it forms a smooth batter.
2. Coarsely crush the sliced almonds into a second shallow dish.
3. Dry the shrimp well with paper towels. Dip into the batter and shake off excess. Transfer to the dish with almonds and coat completely.
4. Place the coated shrimp on a plate or baking sheet and freeze for 1 hour or up to 1 week before air-frying.
5. Preheat the air fryer to 200°C/400°F.
6. Transfer 8 frozen shrimp at a time to the air fryer basket. Air-fry for 6 minutes. Turn and air-fry 4 more minutes. Repeat with remaining shrimp.
7. While shrimp cook, boil amaretto in a saucepan until reduced and thickened into a glaze, about 10 minutes.
8. Remove shrimp and brush both sides with the warm amaretto glaze. Serve warm.

### Variations & Ingredients Tips:

- Use other nuts like pecans or walnuts instead of almonds.
- Add chili powder or cayenne to the batter for some heat.
- Serve over salad greens or with rice pilaf.

**Per Serving:** Calories: 290, Total Fat: 9g, Saturated Fat: 1g, Cholesterol: 235mg, Sodium: 520mg, Total Carbs: 25g, Fiber: 2g, Sugars: 8g, Protein: 23g

## Fish Tacos With Jalapeño-lime Sauce

**Servings: 4 | Prep Time: 15 Minutes | Cooking Time: 7 Minutes**

### Ingredients:

- Fish Tacos:
- 450g fish fillets
- 1/4 teaspoon cumin
- 1/4 teaspoon coriander
- 1/8 teaspoon ground red pepper
- 1 tablespoon lime zest
- 1/4 teaspoon smoked paprika
- 1 teaspoon oil
- Cooking spray
- 6–8 corn or flour tortillas (15-cm size)
- Jalapeño-Lime Sauce:
- 1/2 cup sour cream
- 1 tablespoon lime juice
- 1/4 teaspoon grated lime zest
- 1/2 teaspoon minced jalapeño (flesh only)
- 1/4 teaspoon cumin
- Napa Cabbage Garnish:
- 1 cup shredded Napa cabbage
- 1/4 cup slivered red or green bell pepper
- 1/4 cup slivered onion

### Directions:

1. Slice the fish fillets into strips approximately 25-cm thick.
2. Put the strips into a sealable plastic bag along with the cumin, coriander, red pepper, lime zest, smoked paprika, and oil. Massage seasonings into the fish until evenly distributed.
3. Spray air fryer basket with nonstick cooking spray and place seasoned fish inside.
4. Cook at 200°C/390°F for approximately 5 minutes. Shake basket to distribute fish. Cook an additional 2 minutes, until fish flakes easily.
5. While the fish is cooking, prepare the Jalapeño-Lime Sauce by mixing the sour cream, lime juice, lime zest, jalapeño, and cumin together to make a smooth sauce. Set aside.
6. Mix the cabbage, bell pepper, and onion together and set aside.
7. To warm refrigerated tortillas, wrap in damp paper towels and microwave for 30 to 60 seconds.
8. To serve, spoon some of fish into a warm tortilla. Add one or two tablespoons Napa Cabbage Garnish and drizzle with Jalapeño-Lime Sauce.

### Variations & Ingredients Tips:

- Use shrimp, scallops or calamari instead of fish.
- Add some chopped mango or pineapple to the slaw for sweetness.
- Top with crumbled cotija cheese or queso fresco.

**Per Serving:** Calories: 320; Total Fat: 14g; Saturated Fat: 5g; Cholesterol: 85mg; Sodium: 320mg; Total Carbs: 25g; Dietary Fiber: 3g; Total Sugars: 3g; Protein: 25g

## Buttered Swordfish Steaks

**Servings: 4 | Prep Time: 15 Minutes | Cooking Time: 30 Minutes**

### Ingredients:

- 4 swordfish steaks
- 2 eggs, beaten
- 85 grams melted butter
- ½ cup breadcrumbs
- Black pepper to taste
- 1 tsp dried rosemary
- 1 tsp dried marjoram
- 1 lemon, cut into wedges

### Directions:

1. Preheat air fryer to 180°C/350°F.
2. Place the eggs and melted butter in a bowl and stir thoroughly.
3. Combine the breadcrumbs, rosemary, marjoram, and black pepper in a separate bowl.
4. Dip the swordfish steaks in the beaten eggs, then coat with the crumb mixture.
5. Place the coated fish in the air fryer basket.
6. Air Fry for 12-14 minutes, turning once until the fish is cooked through and the crust is toasted and crispy.
7. Serve with lemon wedges.

### Variations & Ingredients Tips:

- Use cod, halibut, or mahi-mahi instead of swordfish for different fish options.
- Add grated Parmesan cheese or finely chopped nuts to the breading for extra flavor and texture.
- Serve with tartar sauce, garlic aioli, or a side of roasted vegetables.

**Per Serving:** Calories: 420; Total Fat: 27g; Saturated Fat: 15g; Sodium: 330mg; Total Carbohydrates: 11g; Dietary Fiber: 1g; Total Sugars: 1g; Protein: 33g

## Perfect Soft-shelled Crabs

**Servings: 2 | Prep Time: 10 Minutes | Cooking Time: 12 Minutes**

### Ingredients:

- 1/2 cup All-purpose flour
- 1 tablespoon Old Bay seasoning
- 1 Large egg, well beaten
- 1 cup (about 85g) Ground oyster crackers
- 2 (115g) cleaned soft-shelled crabs, about 10cm across
- Vegetable oil spray

### Directions:

1. Preheat the air fryer to 190°C/375°F.
2. Set up three shallow plates: one with flour whisked with Old Bay, one for beaten egg, one for cracker crumbs.
3. Coat a crab in flour, dip in egg, coat in crumbs, pressing gently. Spray generously with oil.
4. Set crab(s) in basket with space between them, may slightly overlap.
5. Air-fry 12 minutes until crisp and golden brown. If 195°C/390°F, may be done in 10 mins.
6. Transfer crab(s) to wire rack and cool briefly before serving.

### Variations & Ingredients Tips:

- Use panko breadcrumbs instead of oyster crackers.
- Substitute Cajun or blackening seasoning for Old Bay.
- Serve with lemon wedges and remoulade sauce.

**Per Serving:** Calories: 350; Total Fat: 10g; Saturated Fat: 3g; Cholesterol: 300mg; Sodium: 1100mg; Total Carbs: 45g; Dietary Fiber: 2g; Sugars: 2g; Protein: 23g

## Home-style Fish Sticks

**Servings: 4 | Prep Time: 15 Minutes | Cooking Time: 30 Minutes**

### Ingredients:

- 450g cod fillets, cut into sticks
- 1 cup flour
- 1 egg
- 1/4 cup cornmeal
- Salt and pepper to taste
- 1/4 tsp smoked paprika
- 1 lemon

### Directions:

1. Preheat air fryer at 175°C/350°F. In a bowl, add 1/2 cup of flour. In another bowl, beat the egg and in a third bowl, combine the remaining flour, cornmeal, salt, black pepper and paprika.
2. Roll the sticks in the flour, shake off excess flour. Then, dip them in the egg, shake off excess egg. Finally, dredge them in the cornmeal mixture.
3. Place fish fingers in the greased frying basket and Air Fry for 10 minutes, flipping once.
4. Serve with squeezed lemon.

### Variations & Ingredients Tips:

- Use haddock, pollock or tilapia instead of cod.
- Substitute cornmeal with panko breadcrumbs for extra crunch.
- Serve with tartar sauce, ketchup or ranch dressing for dipping.

**Per Serving:** Calories: 260; Total Fat: 4g; Saturated Fat: 0.5g; Cholesterol: 100mg; Sodium: 200mg; Total Carbs: 29g; Dietary Fiber: 1g; Total Sugars: 0g; Protein: 28g

## Sweet Potato–wrapped Shrimp

**Servings: 3 | Prep Time: 15 Minutes | Cooking Time: 6 Minutes**

## Ingredients:

- 24 Long spiralized sweet potato strands
- Olive oil spray
- ¼ tsp garlic powder
- ¼ tsp table salt
- Up to a ⅛ tsp cayenne
- 12 Large shrimp (20–25 per g), peeled and deveined

## Directions:

1. Preheat the air fryer to 200°C/400°F.
2. Lay the spiralized sweet potato strands on a large swath of paper towels and straighten out the strands to long ropes. Coat them with olive oil spray, then sprinkle them with the garlic powder, salt, and cayenne.
3. Pick up 2 strands and wrap them around the center of a shrimp, with the ends tucked under what now becomes the bottom side of the shrimp. Continue wrapping the remainder of the shrimp.
4. Set the shrimp bottom side down in the basket with as much air space between them as possible. Air-fry undisturbed for 6 minutes, or until the sweet potato strands are crisp and the shrimp are pink and firm.
5. Use kitchen tongs to transfer the shrimp to a wire rack. Cool for only a minute or two before serving.

## Variations & Ingredients Tips:

- Use zucchini noodles instead of sweet potato for a different flavor and texture.
- Add some paprika or chili powder to the seasoning mix for extra heat.
- Serve with a dipping sauce like sweet chili or garlic aioli.

**Per Serving:** Calories: 120; Total Fat: 1g; Saturated Fat: 0g; Cholesterol: 110mg; Sodium: 420mg; Total Carbohydrates: 12g; Dietary Fiber: 2g; Total Sugars: 3g; Protein: 14g

## Tilapia Al Pesto

**Servings: 4 | Prep Time: 15 Minutes | Cooking Time: 25 Minutes**

### Ingredients:

- 4 tilapia fillets
- 1 egg
- 2 tbsp buttermilk
- 1 cup crushed cornflakes
- Salt and pepper to taste
- 4 tsp pesto
- 2 tbsp butter, melted
- 4 lemon wedges

### Directions:

1. Preheat air fryer to 175°C/350°F.
2. Whisk egg and buttermilk in a bowl. In another bowl, combine cornflakes, salt, and pepper.
3. Spread 1 tsp of pesto on each tilapia fillet, then tightly roll the fillet from one short end to the other. Secure with a toothpick.
4. Dip each fillet in the egg mixture and dredge in the cornflake mixture. Place fillets in the greased frying basket, drizzle with melted butter, and Air Fry for 6 minutes.
5. Let rest onto a serving dish for 5 minutes before removing the toothpicks.
6. Serve with lemon wedges.

### Variations & Ingredients Tips:

- Use cod, sole or flounder instead of tilapia.
- Substitute pesto with sun-dried tomato paste or olive tapenade.
- Serve over a bed of sautéed spinach or roasted vegetables.

**Per Serving:** Calories: 320; Total Fat: 16g; Saturated Fat: 6g; Cholesterol: 110mg; Sodium: 400mg; Total Carbs: 18g; Dietary Fiber: 1g; Total Sugars: 2g; Protein: 28g

## Flounder Fillets

**Servings: 4 | Prep Time: 10 Minutes | Cooking Time: 8 Minutes**

### Ingredients:

- 1 egg white
- 1 tablespoon water
- 1 cup panko breadcrumbs
- 2 tablespoons extra-light virgin olive oil
- 4 (115g) flounder fillets
- Salt and pepper
- Oil for misting or cooking spray

### Directions:

1. Preheat air fryer to 195°C/390°F.
2. Beat together egg white and water in shallow dish.
3. In another shallow dish, mix panko crumbs and oil until well combined and crumbly (best done by hand).
4. Season flounder fillets with salt and pepper to taste. Dip each fillet into egg mixture and then roll in panko crumbs, pressing in crumbs so that fish is nicely coated.
5. Spray air fryer basket with nonstick cooking spray and add fillets. Cook at 195°C/390°F for 3 minutes.
6. Spray fish fillets but do not turn. Cook 5 minutes longer or until golden brown and crispy. Using a spatula, carefully remove fish from basket and serve.

### Variations & Ingredients Tips:

- Use cod, sole or tilapia instead of flounder.
- Add some grated Parmesan or lemon zest to the panko breading.
- Serve with tartar sauce, lemon wedges and steamed vegetables.

**Per Serving:** Calories: 230; Total Fat: 8g; Saturated Fat: 1.5g; Cholesterol: 75mg; Sodium: 300mg; Total Carbs: 13g; Dietary Fiber: 1g; Total Sugars: 1g; Protein: 25g

# Beef, Pork & Lamb Recipes

## Lamb Chops

**Servings: 2 | Prep Time: 5 Minutes (plus Marinating Time) | Cooking Time: 20 Minutes**

**Ingredients:**

- 2 teaspoons oil
- ½ teaspoon ground rosemary
- ½ teaspoon lemon juice
- 450 g lamb chops, approximately 2.5 cm thick
- Salt and pepper
- Cooking spray

**Directions:**

1. Mix the oil, rosemary, and lemon juice together and rub into all sides of the lamb chops. Season to taste with salt and pepper.
2. For best flavor, cover lamb chops and allow them to rest in the fridge for 20 minutes.
3. Spray air fryer basket with nonstick spray and place lamb chops in it.
4. Cook at 180°C/360°F for approximately 20 minutes. This will cook chops to medium. The meat will be juicy but have no remaining pink. Cook for a minute or two longer for well done chops. For rare chops, stop cooking after about 12 minutes and check for doneness.

**Variations & Ingredients Tips:**

- Use different herbs, such as thyme or oregano, for a variety of flavors.
- Add some minced garlic or Dijon mustard to the marinade for extra flavor.
- Serve the lamb chops with a side of roasted vegetables or mashed potatoes for a complete meal.

**Per Serving:** Calories: 450; Total Fat: 32g; Saturated Fat: 13g; Cholesterol: 145mg; Sodium: 130mg; Total Carbs: 0g; Fiber: 0g; Sugars: 0g; Protein: 38g

## Barbecue-style London Broil

**Servings: 5 | Prep Time: 5 Minutes | Cooking Time: 17 Minutes**

**Ingredients:**

- ¾ tsp mild smoked paprika
- ¾ tsp dried oregano
- ¾ tsp table salt
- ¾ tsp ground black pepper
- ¼ tsp garlic powder
- ¼ tsp onion powder
- 680 g beef London broil (in one piece)
- Olive oil spray

**Directions:**

1. Preheat the air fryer to 200°C/400°F. Mix the smoked paprika, oregano, salt, pepper, garlic powder, and onion powder in a small bowl until uniform. Pat and rub this mixture across all surfaces of the beef. Lightly coat the beef on all sides with olive oil spray. When the machine is at temperature, lay the London broil flat in the basket and air-fry undisturbed for 8 minutes for the small batch, 10 minutes for the medium batch, or 12 minutes for the large batch for medium-rare, until an instant-read meat thermometer inserted into the center of the meat registers 55°C/130°F (not USDA-approved). Add 1, 2, or 3 minutes, respectively (based on the size of the cut) for medium, until an instant-read meat thermometer registers 57°C/135°F (not USDA-approved). Or add 3, 4, or 5 minutes respectively for medium, until an instant-read meat thermometer registers 63°C/145°F (USDA-approved). Use kitchen tongs to transfer the London broil to a cutting board. Let the meat rest for 10 minutes. It needs a long time for the juices to be reincorporated into the meat's fibers. Carve it against the grain into very thin (less than 6-mm-thick) slices to serve.

**Variations & Ingredients Tips:**

- Marinate the beef in a mixture of soy sauce, Worcestershire sauce, olive oil, and garlic for extra flavor.
- Slice the cooked London broil and serve in sandwiches, salads, or wraps.
- Brush with chimichurri sauce or horseradish cream sauce before serving for a bright, tangy finish.

**Per Serving:** Calories: 213; Total Fat: 10g; Saturated Fat: 4g; Cholesterol: 74mg; Sodium: 416mg; Total Carbohydrates: 1g; Dietary Fiber: 0g; Total Sugars: 0g; Protein: 28g

## Canadian-style Rib Eye Steak

**Servings: 2 | Prep Time: 5 Minutes | Cooking Time: 15 Minutes**

**Ingredients:**

- 2 teaspoons Montreal steak seasoning
- 1 ribeye steak
- 1 tablespoon butter, halved
- 1 teaspoon chopped parsley
- 1/2 teaspoon fresh rosemary

**Directions:**

1. Preheat air fryer at 205°C/400°F. Sprinkle ribeye with steak seasoning and rosemary on both sides. Place it in the basket and Bake for 10 minutes, turning once. Remove it

to a cutting board and top with butter halves. Let rest for 5 minutes and scatter with parsley. Serve immediately.

**Variations & Ingredients Tips:**

- Let the steak come to room temperature before cooking for more even cooking
- Try different steak rubs or seasonings like garlic powder, paprika or coffee rub
- For extra richness, baste the steak with melted butter or beef broth while resting

**Per Serving:** Calories: 430; Total Fat: 30g; Saturated Fat: 14g; Cholesterol: 135mg; Sodium: 310mg; Total Carbs: 1g; Dietary Fiber: 0g; Total Sugars: 0g; Protein: 37g

## Chinese-style Lamb Chops

**Servings: 4 | Prep Time: 10 Minutes (plus Marinating Time) | Cooking Time: 25 Minutes**

**Ingredients:**

- 8 lamb chops, trimmed
- 2 tablespoons scallions, sliced
- ¼ teaspoon Chinese five-spice
- 3 garlic cloves, crushed
- ½ teaspoon ginger powder
- ¼ cup dark soy sauce
- 2 teaspoons orange juice
- 3 tablespoons honey
- ½ tablespoon light brown sugar
- ¼ teaspoon red pepper flakes

**Directions:**

1. Season the chops with garlic, ginger, soy sauce, five-spice powder, orange juice, and honey in a bowl. Toss to coat. Cover the bowl with plastic wrap and marinate for 2 hours and up to overnight.
2. Preheat air fryer to 200°C/400°F. Remove the chops from the bowl but reserve the marinade. Place the chops in the greased frying basket and Bake for 5 minutes. Using tongs, flip the chops. Brush the lamb with the reserved marinade, then sprinkle with brown sugar and pepper flakes. Cook for another 4 minutes until brown and caramelized medium-rare. Serve with scallions on top.

**Variations & Ingredients Tips:**

- Use different types of meat, such as pork or chicken, for a variety of flavors and textures.
- Add some minced garlic or ginger to the marinade for extra flavor.
- Serve the lamb chops with a side of stir-fried vegetables or rice for a complete meal.

**Per Serving:** Calories: 380; Total Fat: 21g; Saturated Fat: 8g; Cholesterol: 105mg; Sodium: 1020mg; Total Carbs: 20g; Fiber: 0g; Sugars: 18g; Protein: 30g

## Stuffed Pork Chops

**Servings: 4 | Prep Time: 10 Minutes | Cooking Time: 12 Minutes**

**Ingredients:**

- 4 boneless pork chops
- ½ teaspoon salt
- ½ teaspoon black pepper
- ¼ teaspoon paprika
- 1 cup frozen spinach, defrosted and squeezed dry
- 2 cloves garlic, minced
- 57 g cream cheese
- 28 g grated Parmesan cheese
- 1 tablespoon extra-virgin olive oil

**Directions:**

1. Pat the pork chops with a paper towel. Make a slit in the side of each pork chop to create a pouch.
2. Season the pork chops with the salt, pepper, and paprika.
3. In a small bowl, mix together the spinach, garlic, cream cheese, and Parmesan cheese.
4. Divide the mixture into fourths and stuff the pork chop pouches. Secure the pouches with toothpicks.
5. Preheat the air fryer to 200°C/400°F.
6. Place the stuffed pork chops in the air fryer basket and spray liberally with cooking spray. Cook for 6 minutes, flip and coat with more cooking spray, and cook another 6 minutes. Check to make sure the meat is cooked to an internal temperature of 63°C/145°F. Cook the pork chops in batches, as needed.

**Variations & Ingredients Tips:**

- Use kale, chard or arugula instead of spinach
- Add some diced sun-dried tomatoes or roasted red peppers to the filling
- Wrap the stuffed chops with prosciutto or bacon before air frying

**Per Serving:** Calories: 288; Total Fat: 17g; Saturated Fat: 7g; Cholesterol: 100mg; Sodium: 521mg; Total Carbs: 3g; Dietary Fiber: 1g; Total Sugars: 1g; Protein: 32g

## Pretzel-coated Pork Tenderloin

**Servings: 4 | Prep Time: 10 Minutes | Cooking Time: 10 Minutes**

**Ingredients:**

- 1 Large egg white(s)
- 2 teaspoons Dijon mustard (gluten-free, if a concern)
- 1½ cups (about 170 g) Crushed pretzel crumbs (see the headnote; gluten-free, if a concern)
- 454 g (4 sections) Pork tenderloin, cut into 113 g sections
- Vegetable oil spray

**Directions:**

1. Preheat the air fryer to 175°C/350°F.
2. Set up and fill two shallow soup plates or small pie plates on your counter: one for the egg white(s), whisked with the mustard until foamy; and one for the pretzel crumbs.
3. Dip a section of pork tenderloin in the egg white mixture and turn it to coat well, even on the ends. Let any excess egg white mixture slip back into the rest, then set the pork in the pretzel crumbs. Roll it several times, pressing gently, until the pork is evenly coated, even on the ends. Generously coat the pork section with vegetable oil spray, set it aside, and continue coating and spraying the remaining sections.
4. Set the pork sections in the basket with at least 6 mm between them. Air-fry undisturbed for 10 minutes, or until an instant-read meat thermometer inserted into the center of one section registers 63°C/145°F.
5. Use kitchen tongs to transfer the pieces to a wire rack. Cool for 3 to 5 minutes before serving.

### Variations & Ingredients Tips:

- Use crushed cornflakes or panko breadcrumbs instead of pretzels
- Add some smoked paprika or cayenne pepper to the crumbs for a spicy kick
- Serve with honey mustard or sweet chili sauce for dipping

**Per Serving:** Calories: 304; Total Fat: 8g; Saturated Fat: 2g; Cholesterol: 100mg; Sodium: 620mg; Total Carbs: 15g; Dietary Fiber: 1g; Total Sugars: 1g; Protein: 39g

## Chorizo & Veggie Bake

**Servings: 4 | Prep Time: 15 Minutes | Cooking Time: 40 Minutes**

### Ingredients:

- 1 cup halved Brussels sprouts
- 450 g baby potatoes, halved
- 1 cup baby carrots
- 1 onion, sliced
- 2 garlic cloves, sliced
- 2 tablespoons olive oil
- Salt and pepper to taste
- 450 g chorizo sausages, sliced
- 2 tablespoons Dijon mustard

### Directions:

1. Preheat the air fryer to 190°C/370°F. Put the potatoes, Brussels sprouts, baby carrots, garlic, and onion in the frying basket and drizzle with olive oil. Sprinkle with salt and pepper; toss to coat.
2. Bake for 15 minutes or until the veggies are crisp but tender, shaking once during cooking.
3. Add the chorizo sausages to the fryer and cook for 8-12 minutes, shaking once until the sausages are hot and the veggies tender.
4. Drizzle with the mustard to serve.

### Variations & Ingredients Tips:

- Use different types of sausage, such as Italian or bratwurst, for a variety of flavors.
- Add some bell peppers or zucchini to the vegetable mixture for extra color and nutrients.
- Serve the chorizo and veggie bake with a side of crusty bread or rice for a complete meal.

**Per Serving:** Calories: 610; Total Fat: 46g; Saturated Fat: 15g; Cholesterol: 85mg; Sodium: 1180mg; Total Carbs: 28g; Fiber: 5g; Sugars: 5g; Protein: 24g

## Greek Pork Chops

**Servings: 4 | Prep Time: 10 Minutes | Cooking Time: 30 Minutes**

### Ingredients:

- 3 tbsp grated Halloumi cheese
- 4 pork chops
- 1 tsp Greek seasoning
- Salt and pepper to taste
- ¼ cup all-purpose flour
- 2 tbsp bread crumbs

### Directions:

1. Preheat air fryer to 190°C/380°F. Season the pork chops with Greek seasoning, salt and pepper. In a shallow bowl, add flour. In another shallow bowl, combine the crumbs and Halloumi. Dip the chops in the flour, then in the bread crumbs. Place them in the fryer and spray with cooking oil. Bake for 12-14 minutes, flipping once. Serve warm.

### Variations & Ingredients Tips:

- Use feta cheese instead of Halloumi for a tangier flavor
- Add some dried herbs like oregano or thyme to the breading mixture
- Serve with a Greek salad and lemon potatoes

**Per Serving:** Calories: 277; Total Fat: 14g; Saturated Fat: 6g; Cholesterol: 80mg; Sodium: 417mg; Total Carbs: 10g; Dietary Fiber: 0g; Total Sugars: 0g; Protein: 28g

## Sloppy Joes

**Servings: 4 | Prep Time: 10 Minutes | Cooking Time: 17 Minutes**

### Ingredients:

- oil for misting or cooking spray
- 454 g very lean ground beef
- 1 teaspoon onion powder
- ⅓ cup ketchup
- ¼ cup water
- ½ teaspoon celery seed
- 1 tablespoon lemon juice
- 1½ teaspoons brown sugar
- 1¼ teaspoons low-sodium Worcestershire sauce
- ½ teaspoon salt (optional)

- ½ teaspoon vinegar
- ⅛ teaspoon dry mustard
- hamburger or slider buns

### Directions:

1. Spray air fryer basket with nonstick cooking spray or olive oil.
2. Break raw ground beef into small chunks and pile into basket.
3. Cook at 195°C/390°F for 5 minutes. Stir to break apart and cook 3 minutes. Stir and cook 4 minutes longer or until meat is well done.
4. Remove meat from air fryer, drain, and use a knife and fork to crumble into small pieces.
5. Give your air fryer basket a quick rinse to remove any bits of meat.
6. Place all the remaining ingredients except the buns in a 15 x 15 cm baking pan and mix together.
7. Add meat and stir well.
8. Cook at 165°C/330°F for 5 minutes. Stir and cook for 2 minutes.
9. Scoop onto buns.

### Variations & Ingredients Tips:

- Use ground turkey or chicken for a lighter version
- Add diced bell peppers, carrots or zucchini to the meat mixture for extra veggies
- Top with sliced cheese, pickles or coleslaw for crunch and flavor

**Per Serving:** Calories: 325; Total Fat: 15g; Saturated Fat: 5g; Cholesterol: 81mg; Sodium: 632mg; Total Carbs: 19g; Dietary Fiber: 1g; Total Sugars: 9g; Protein: 28g

## Crispy Pierogi With Kielbasa And Onions

**Servings: 3 | Prep Time: 5 Minutes | Cooking Time: 20 Minutes**

### Ingredients:

- 6 frozen potato and cheese pierogi, thawed (about 12 pierogi to 450 g)
- 225 g smoked kielbasa, sliced into 1.25 cm thick rounds
- ¾ cup very roughly chopped sweet onion, preferably Vidalia
- Vegetable oil spray

### Directions:

1. Preheat the air fryer to 190°C/375°F.
2. Put the pierogi, kielbasa rounds, and onion in a large bowl. Coat them with vegetable oil spray, toss well, spray again, and toss until everything is glistening.
3. When the machine is at temperature, dump the contents of the bowl it into the basket. (Items may be leaning against each other and even on top of each other.) Air-fry, tossing and rearranging everything twice so that all covered surfaces get exposed, for 20 minutes, or until the sausages have begun to brown and the pierogi are crisp.
4. Pour the contents of the basket onto a serving platter. Wait a minute or two just to take make sure nothing's searing hot before serving.

### Variations & Ingredients Tips:

- Use different types of pierogi, such as sauerkraut or mushroom, for a variety of flavors.
- Add some sliced bell peppers or zucchini to the pierogi mixture for extra vegetables.
- Serve the pierogi with a side of sour cream or applesauce for a classic pairing.

**Per Serving:** Calories: 440; Total Fat: 26g; Saturated Fat: 9g; Cholesterol: 65mg; Sodium: 1120mg; Total Carbs: 35g; Fiber: 2g; Sugars: 5g; Protein: 17g

## Lamb Meatballs With Quick Tomato Sauce

**Servings: 4 | Prep Time: 20 Minutes | Cooking Time: 8 Minutes**

### Ingredients:

- ½ small onion, finely diced
- 1 clove garlic, minced
- 450 g ground lamb
- 2 tablespoons fresh parsley, finely chopped (plus more for garnish)
- 2 teaspoons fresh oregano, finely chopped
- 2 tablespoons milk
- 1 egg yolk
- Salt and freshly ground black pepper
- ½ cup crumbled feta cheese, for garnish
- Tomato Sauce:
- 2 tablespoons butter
- 1 clove garlic, smashed
- Pinch crushed red pepper flakes
- ¼ teaspoon ground cinnamon
- 1 (800 g) can crushed tomatoes
- Salt, to taste

### Directions:

1. Combine all ingredients for the meatballs in a large bowl and mix just until everything is combined. Shape the mixture into 4 cm balls or shape the meat between two spoons to make quenelles (little three-sided footballs).
2. Preheat the air fryer to 200°C/400°F.
3. While the air fryer is preheating, start the quick tomato sauce. Place the butter, garlic and red pepper flakes in a sauté pan and heat over medium heat on the stovetop. Let the garlic sizzle a little, but before the butter starts to brown, add the cinnamon and tomatoes. Bring to a simmer and simmer for 15 minutes. Season to taste with salt (but not too much as the feta that you will be sprinkling on at the end will be salty).
4. Brush the bottom of the air fryer basket with a little oil and transfer the meatballs to the air fryer basket in one lay-

er, air-frying in batches if necessary.
5. Air-fry at 200°C/400°F for 8 minutes, giving the basket a shake once during the cooking process to turn the meatballs over.
6. To serve, spoon a pool of the tomato sauce onto plates and add the meatballs in a decorative manner. Sprinkle the feta cheese on top and garnish with more fresh parsley. Serve immediately.

### Variations & Ingredients Tips:

- Use different types of cheese, such as goat cheese or Parmesan, for a variety of flavors.
- Add some chopped Kalamata olives or capers to the tomato sauce for a briny flavor.
- Serve the meatballs with a side of pasta or crusty bread for a complete meal.

**Per Serving:** Calories: 510; Total Fat: 38g; Saturated Fat: 18g; Cholesterol: 170mg; Sodium: 780mg; Total Carbs: 15g; Fiber: 3g; Sugars: 8g; Protein: 31g

## Honey Mesquite Pork Chops

**Servings: 2 | Prep Time: 5 Minutes | Cooking Time: 10 Minutes**

### Ingredients:

- 2 tbsp mesquite seasoning
- ¼ cup honey
- 1 tbsp olive oil
- 1 tbsp water
- freshly ground black pepper
- 2 bone-in center cut pork chops (about 454 g)

### Directions:

1. Whisk the mesquite seasoning, honey, olive oil, water and freshly ground black pepper together in a shallow glass dish. Pierce the chops all over and on both sides with a fork or meat tenderizer. Add the pork chops to the marinade and massage the marinade into the chops. Cover and marinate for 30 minutes.
2. Preheat the air fryer to 165°C/330°F.
3. Transfer the pork chops to the air fryer basket and pour half of the marinade over the chops, reserving the remaining marinade. Air-fry the pork chops for 6 minutes. Flip the pork chops over and pour the remaining marinade on top. Air-fry for an additional 3 minutes at 165°C/330°F. Then, increase the air fryer temperature to 200°C/400°F and air-fry the pork chops for an additional minute.
4. Transfer the pork chops to a serving plate, and let them rest for 5 minutes before serving. If you'd like a sauce for these chops, pour the cooked marinade from the bottom of the air fryer over the top.

### Variations & Ingredients Tips:

- Try different spice rubs like cajun, jerk or five-spice powder
- Substitute the honey with maple syrup or brown sugar
- Serve with grilled pineapple or peach slices for a sweet-savory combo

**Per Serving:** Calories: 381; Total Fat: 18g; Saturated Fat: 4g; Cholesterol: 103mg; Sodium: 1148mg; Total Carbs: 25g; Dietary Fiber: 0g; Total Sugars: 24g; Protein: 31g

## Sausage-cheese Calzone

**Servings: 8 | Prep Time: 25 Minutes | Cooking Time: 8 Minutes**

### Ingredients:

- Crust
- 2 cups white wheat flour, plus more for kneading and rolling
- 1 package (7 g) Rapid-Rise yeast
- 1 teaspoon salt
- ½ teaspoon dried basil
- 1 cup warm water (46°C to 52°C)
- 2 teaspoons olive oil
- Filling
- 113 g Italian sausage
- ½ cup ricotta cheese
- 113 g mozzarella cheese, shredded
- ¼ cup grated Parmesan cheese
- oil for misting or cooking spray
- marinara sauce for serving

### Directions:

1. Crumble Italian sausage into air fryer baking pan and cook at 200°C/390°F for 5 minutes. Stir, breaking apart, and cook for 3 to 4 minutes, until well done. Remove and set aside on paper towels to drain.
2. To make dough, combine flour, yeast, salt, and basil. Add warm water and oil and stir until a soft dough forms. Turn out onto lightly floured board and knead for 3 or 4 minutes. Let dough rest for 10 minutes.
3. To make filling, combine the three cheeses in a medium bowl and mix well. Stir in the cooked sausage.
4. Cut dough into 8 pieces.
5. Working with 4 pieces of the dough, press each into a circle about 12.5 cm in diameter. Top each dough circle with 2 heaping tablespoons of filling. Fold over to create a half-moon shape and press edges firmly together. Be sure that edges are firmly sealed to prevent leakage. Spray both sides with oil or cooking spray.
6. Place 4 calzones in air fryer basket and cook at 180°C/360°F for 5 minutes. Mist with oil and cook for 3 minutes, until crust is done and nicely browned.
7. While the first batch is cooking, press out the remaining dough, fill, and shape into calzones.
8. Spray both sides with oil and cook for 5 minutes. If needed, mist with oil and continue cooking for 3 minutes longer. This second batch will cook a little faster than the first because your air fryer is already hot.
9. Serve with marinara sauce on the side for dipping.

### Variations & Ingredients Tips:

- Use pepperoni, ham or cooked veggies for the filling
- Brush the calzones with garlic butter before air frying
- Sprinkle with Italian seasoning or crushed red pepper flakes before serving

**Per Serving:** Calories: 254; Total Fat: 10g; Saturated Fat: 5g; Cholesterol: 26mg; Sodium: 494mg; Total Carbs: 29g; Dietary Fiber: 3g; Total Sugars: 1g; Protein: 12g

## Pork Cutlets With Aloha Salsa

**Servings: 4 | Prep Time: 20 Minutes | Cooking Time: 9 Minutes**

### Ingredients:

- Aloha Salsa
- 1 cup fresh pineapple, chopped in small pieces
- ¼ cup red onion, finely chopped
- ¼ cup green or red bell pepper, chopped
- ½ teaspoon ground cinnamon
- 1 teaspoon low-sodium soy sauce
- ⅛ teaspoon crushed red pepper
- ⅛ teaspoon ground black pepper
- 2 eggs
- 2 tablespoons milk
- ¼ cup flour
- ¼ cup panko breadcrumbs
- 4 teaspoons sesame seeds
- 454 g boneless, thin pork cutlets (1 cm to 1.3 cm thick)
- lemon pepper and salt
- ¼ cup cornstarch
- oil for misting or cooking spray

### Directions:

1. In a medium bowl, stir together all ingredients for salsa. Cover and refrigerate while cooking pork.
2. Preheat air fryer to 200°C/390°F.
3. Beat together eggs and milk in shallow dish.
4. In another shallow dish, mix together the flour, panko, and sesame seeds.
5. Sprinkle pork cutlets with lemon pepper and salt to taste. Most lemon pepper seasoning contains salt, so go easy adding extra.
6. Dip pork cutlets in cornstarch, egg mixture, and then panko coating. Spray both sides with oil or cooking spray.
7. Cook cutlets for 3 minutes. Turn cutlets over, spraying both sides, and continue cooking for 6 minutes or until well done.
8. Serve fried cutlets with salsa on the side.

### Variations & Ingredients Tips:

- Use chicken cutlets or thin slices of firm tofu for a change
- Add some shredded coconut to the breading for a tropical twist
- Serve with steamed rice and stir-fried veggies on the side

**Per Serving:** Calories: 428; Total Fat: 15g; Saturated Fat: 4g; Cholesterol: 168mg; Sodium: 558mg; Total Carbs: 39g; Dietary Fiber: 3g; Total Sugars: 11g; Protein: 35g

## Tender Steak With Salsa Verde

**Servings: 4 | Prep Time: 10 Minutes | Cooking Time: 20 Minutes**

### Ingredients:

- 1 flank steak (around 680g), halved
- 1 ½ cups salsa verde
- ½ tsp black pepper

### Directions:

1. Toss steak and 1 cup of salsa verde in a bowl and refrigerate covered for 2 hours.
2. Preheat air fryer to 400°F/205°C.
3. Add steaks to the lightly greased frying basket and Air Fry for 10-12 minutes or until you reach your desired doneness, flipping once.
4. Let sit onto a cutting board for 5 minutes.
5. Thinly slice against the grain and divide between 4 plates.
6. Spoon over the remaining salsa verde and serve sprinkled with black pepper.

### Variations & Ingredients Tips:

- Use skirt or hanger steak instead of flank steak
- Make your own salsa verde for fresher flavor
- Add sliced avocado or crumbled queso fresco as a topping

**Per Serving:** Calories: 250; Total Fat: 14g; Saturated Fat: 4g; Cholesterol: 65mg; Sodium: 300mg; Total Carbs: 2g; Dietary Fiber: 1g; Total Sugars: 1g; Protein: 27g

## Peachy Pork Chops

**Servings: 2 | Prep Time: 35 Minutes | Cooking Time: 20 Minutes**

### Ingredients:

- 2 tablespoons peach preserves
- 2 tablespoons tomato paste
- 1 tablespoon Dijon mustard
- 1 teaspoon BBQ sauce
- 1 tablespoon lime juice
- 1 tablespoon olive oil
- 2 cloves garlic, minced
- 2 pork chops

### Directions:

1. Whisk all ingredients in a bowl until well mixed and let chill covered in the fridge for 30 minutes.
2. Preheat air fryer to 180°C/350°F. Place pork chops in the frying basket and Air Fry for 12 minutes or until cooked through and tender.
3. Transfer the chops to a cutting board and let sit for 5 minutes before serving.

### Variations & Ingredients Tips:

- Use different types of fruit preserves, such as apricot or

mango, for a variety of flavors.
- Add some chopped fresh herbs, such as thyme or rosemary, to the marinade for extra flavor.
- Serve the pork chops with a side of grilled peaches or a peach salsa for a fruity twist.

**Per Serving:** Calories: 320; Total Fat: 16g; Saturated Fat: 4g; Cholesterol: 90mg; Sodium: 520mg; Total Carbs: 16g; Fiber: 1g; Sugars: 12g; Protein: 29g

## Barbecue-style Beef Cube Steak

**Servings: 2 | Prep Time: 10 Minutes | Cooking Time: 14 Minutes**

### Ingredients:

- 2 115-g beef cube steaks
- 2 cups (about 225 g) Fritos (original flavor) or a generic corn chip equivalent, crushed to crumbs (see here)
- 6 tbsp purchased smooth barbecue sauce, any flavor (gluten-free, if a concern)

### Directions:

1. Preheat the air fryer to 190°C/375°F. Spread the Fritos crumbs in a shallow soup plate or a small pie plate. Rub the barbecue sauce onto both sides of the steaks. Dredge the steaks in the Fritos crumbs to coat well and thoroughly, turning several times and pressing down to get the little bits to adhere to the meat. When the machine is at temperature, set the steaks in the basket. Leave as much air space between them as possible if you're working with more than one piece of beef. Air-fry undisturbed for 12 minutes, or until lightly brown and crunchy. If the machine is at 180°C/360°F, you may need to add 2 minutes to the cooking time. Use kitchen tongs to transfer the steaks to a wire rack. Cool for 5 minutes before serving.

### Variations & Ingredients Tips:

- Use panko breadcrumbs or crushed potato chips instead of Fritos for a different crunchy coating.
- Brush the steaks with honey mustard, teriyaki sauce, or hot sauce before coating for varied flavors.
- Serve with mashed potatoes, coleslaw, or baked beans for a complete meal.

**Per Serving:** Calories: 460; Total Fat: 21g; Saturated Fat: 4g; Cholesterol: 77mg; Sodium: 1024mg; Total Carbohydrates: 38g; Dietary Fiber: 2g; Total Sugars: 17g; Protein: 30g

## Original Köttbullar

**Servings: 4 | Prep Time: 15 Minutes | Cooking Time: 30 Minutes**

### Ingredients:

- 450 g ground beef
- 1 small onion, chopped
- 1 clove garlic, minced
- ⅓ cup bread crumbs
- 1 egg, beaten
- Salt and pepper to taste
- 1 cup beef broth
- ⅓ cup heavy cream
- 2 tablespoons flour

### Directions:

1. Preheat air fryer to 190°C/370°F. Combine beef, onion, garlic, crumbs, egg, salt and pepper in a bowl. Scoop 2 tablespoons of mixture and form meatballs with hands.
2. Place the meatballs in the greased frying basket. Bake for 14 minutes.
3. Meanwhile, stir-fry beef broth and heavy cream in a saucepan over medium heat for 2 minutes; stir in flour. Cover and simmer for 4 minutes or until the sauce thicken.
4. Transfer meatballs to a serving dish and drizzle with sauce. Serve and enjoy!

### Variations & Ingredients Tips:

- Use different types of ground meat, such as pork or turkey, for a variety of flavors.
- Add some grated nutmeg or cardamom to the meatball mixture for a traditional Swedish flavor.
- Serve the meatballs with a side of mashed potatoes or lingonberry jam for an authentic Swedish meal.

**Per Serving:** Calories: 420; Total Fat: 29g; Saturated Fat: 13g; Cholesterol: 155mg; Sodium: 570mg; Total Carbs: 12g; Fiber: 1g; Sugars: 2g; Protein: 29g

## Classic Beef Meatballs

**Servings: 4 | Prep Time: 15 Minutes | Cooking Time: 30 Minutes**

### Ingredients:

- 3 tablespoons buttermilk
- ⅓ cup bread crumbs
- 1 tablespoon ketchup
- 1 egg
- ½ teaspoon dried marjoram
- Salt and pepper to taste
- 450 g ground beef
- 20 Swiss cheese cubes

### Directions:

1. Preheat air fryer to 200°C/390°F.
2. Mix buttermilk, crumbs, ketchup, egg, marjoram, salt, and pepper in a bowl.
3. Using your hands, mix in ground beef until just combined.
4. Shape into 20 meatballs. Take one meatball and shape it around a Swiss cheese cube. Repeat this for the remaining meatballs.
5. Lightly spray the meatballs with oil and place into the frying basket.
6. Bake the meatballs for 10-13 minutes, turning once until they are cooked through.
7. Serve and enjoy!

**Variations & Ingredients Tips:**

- Use different types of cheese, such as cheddar or mozzarella, for a variety of flavors.
- Add some minced garlic or onion to the meatball mixture for extra flavor.
- Serve the meatballs with a side of tomato sauce or gravy for a classic pairing.

**Per Serving:** Calories: 380; Total Fat: 25g; Saturated Fat: 11g; Cholesterol: 145mg; Sodium: 360mg; Total Carbs: 10g; Fiber: 0g; Sugars: 2g; Protein: 29g

## Pork Tenderloin With Apples & Celery

**Servings: 4 | Prep Time: 10 Minutes | Cooking Time: 30 Minutes**

**Ingredients:**

- 454 g pork tenderloin, cut into 4 pieces
- 2 Granny Smith apples, sliced
- 1 tablespoon butter, melted
- 2 teaspoons olive oil
- 3 celery stalks, sliced
- 1 onion, sliced
- 2 teaspoons dried thyme
- 1/3 cup apple juice

**Directions:**

1. Preheat air fryer to 200°C/400°F. Brush olive oil and butter all over the pork, then toss the pork, apples, celery, onion, thyme, and apple juice in a bowl and mix well. Put the bowl in the air fryer and Roast for 15-19 minutes until the pork is cooked through and the apples and veggies are soft, stirring once during cooking. Serve warm.

**Variations & Ingredients Tips:**

- Use pears or peaches instead of apples for a different flavor
- Add some chopped sage or rosemary to the herb mixture
- Serve with mashed sweet potatoes or roasted Brussels sprouts

**Per Serving:** Calories: 277; Total Fat: 10g; Saturated Fat: 3g; Cholesterol: 83mg; Sodium: 85mg; Total Carbs: 17g; Dietary Fiber: 3g; Total Sugars: 12g; Protein: 30g

# Appetizers And Snacks

## Tomato & Garlic Roasted Potatoes

**Servings: 4 | Prep Time: 10 Minutes | Cooking Time: 25 Minutes**

**Ingredients:**

- 16 cherry tomatoes, halved
- 6 red potatoes, cubed
- 3 garlic cloves, minced
- Salt and pepper to taste
- 1 tsp chopped chives
- 1 tbsp extra-virgin olive oil

**Directions:**

1. Preheat air fryer to 190°C/370°F. Combine cherry potatoes, garlic, salt, pepper, chives and olive oil in a resealable plastic bag. Seal and shake the bag. Put the potatoes in the greased frying basket and roast for 10 minutes. Shake the basket, place the cherry tomatoes in, and cook for 10 more minutes. Allow to cool slightly and serve.

**Variations & Ingredients Tips:**

- Add chopped rosemary, thyme, or oregano for an herbal flavor.
- Sprinkle with grated Parmesan cheese or nutritional yeast after cooking for a cheesy taste.
- Serve with a side of aioli, ranch dressing, or sour cream for dipping.

**Per Serving:** Calories: 158; Total Fat: 4g; Saturated Fat: 1g; Sodium: 16mg; Total Carbohydrates: 28g; Dietary Fiber: 4g; Total Sugars: 3g; Protein: 4g

## Sweet-and-salty Pretzels

**Servings: 4 | Prep Time: 5 Minutes | Cooking Time: 5 Minutes**

**Ingredients:**

- 2 cups plain pretzel nuggets
- 1 tbsp Worcestershire sauce
- 2 tsp granulated white sugar
- 1 tsp mild smoked paprika
- ½ tsp garlic or onion powder

**Directions:**

1. Preheat the air fryer to 175°C/350°F. Put the pretzel nuggets, Worcestershire sauce, sugar, smoked paprika, and garlic or onion powder in a large bowl. Toss gently until the nuggets are well coated. When the machine is at temperature, pour the nuggets into the basket, spreading them into as close to a single layer as possible. Air-fry, shaking the basket three or four times to rearrange the nuggets, for 5 minutes, or until the nuggets are toasted and aromatic. Although the coating will darken, don't let it burn, especially if the machine's temperature is 180°C/360°F. Pour the nuggets onto a wire rack and gently spread them into one layer. (A rubber spatula does a good job.) Cool for 5 minutes before serving.

### Variations & Ingredients Tips:

- Experiment with different spice blends like ranch seasoning, taco seasoning, or Italian herbs.
- Add a pinch of cayenne pepper or red pepper flakes for a spicy kick.
- Drizzle with melted chocolate or caramel for a sweet and salty treat.

**Per Serving:** Calories: 113; Total Fat: 1g; Saturated Fat: 0g; Sodium: 504mg; Total Carbohydrates: 24g; Dietary Fiber: 1g; Total Sugars: 3g; Protein: 3g

## Mediterranean Potato Skins

**Servings: 4 | Prep Time: 10 Minutes | Cooking Time: 50 Minutes**

### Ingredients:

- 2 russet potatoes
- 3 tbsp olive oil
- Salt and pepper to taste
- 2 tbsp rosemary, chopped
- 10 Kalamata olives, diced
- ¼ cup crumbled feta
- 2 tbsp chopped dill

### Directions:

1. Preheat air fryer to 190°C/380°F. Poke 2-3 holes in the potatoes with a fork. Drizzle them with some olive oil and sprinkle with salt. Put the potatoes into the frying basket and bake for 30 minutes. When the potatoes are ready, remove them from the fryer and slice in half. Scoop out the flesh of the potatoes with a spoon, leaving a 3-cm layer of potato inside the skins, and set the skins aside. Combine the scooped potato middles with the remaining olive oil, salt, black pepper, and rosemary in a medium bowl. Mix until well combined. Spoon the potato filling into the potato skins, spreading it evenly over them. Top with olives, dill, and feta. Put the loaded potato skins back into the air fryer and bake for 15 minutes. Enjoy!

### Variations & Ingredients Tips:

- Add sun-dried tomatoes, artichokes, or roasted red peppers for more Mediterranean flavors.
- Substitute feta with goat cheese or ricotta salata for a different taste.
- Sprinkle with smoked paprika or red pepper flakes for a spicy kick.

**Per Serving:** Calories: 257; Total Fat: 18g; Saturated Fat: 4g; Cholesterol: 17mg; Sodium: 327mg; Total Carbs: 21g; Dietary Fiber: 2g; Total Sugars: 1g; Protein: 5g

## Spicy Chicken And Pepper Jack Cheese Bites

**Servings: 8 | Prep Time: 20 Minutes + Chilling Time | Cooking Time: 8 Minutes**

### Ingredients:

- 225 g cream cheese, softened
- 2 cups grated pepper jack cheese
- 1 jalapeño pepper, diced
- 2 scallions, minced
- 1 tsp paprika
- 2 tsp salt, divided
- 3 cups shredded cooked chicken
- ¼ cup all-purpose flour*
- 2 eggs, lightly beaten
- 1 cup panko breadcrumbs*
- olive oil, in a spray bottle
- salsa

### Directions:

1. Beat the cream cheese in a bowl until it is smooth and easy to stir. Add the pepper jack cheese, jalapeño pepper, scallions, paprika and 1 teaspoon of salt. Fold in the shredded cooked chicken and combine well. Roll this mixture into 2.5-cm balls. Set up a dredging station with three shallow dishes. Place the flour into one shallow dish. Place the eggs into a second shallow dish. Finally, combine the panko breadcrumbs and remaining teaspoon of salt in a third dish. Coat the chicken cheese balls by rolling each ball in the flour first, then dip them into the eggs and finally roll them in the panko breadcrumbs to coat all sides. Refrigerate for at least 30 minutes. Preheat the air fryer to 200°C/400°F. Spray the chicken cheese balls with oil and air-fry in batches for 8 minutes. Shake the basket a few times throughout the cooking process to help the balls brown evenly. Serve hot with salsa on the side.

### Variations & Ingredients Tips:

- Use a mixture of cheddar, mozzarella, and Parmesan cheese for a milder flavor.
- Add chopped bacon, ham, or chorizo for a meatier bite.
- Serve with ranch dressing, honey mustard, or BBQ sauce for dipping.

**Per Serving:** Calories: 341; Total Fat: 24g; Saturated Fat: 12g; Cholesterol: 143mg; Sodium: 892mg; Total Carbohydrates: 9g; Dietary Fiber: 1g; Total Sugars: 1g; Protein: 23g

## Beef Steak Sliders

**Servings: 8 | Prep Time: 10 Minutes | Cooking Time: 22 Minutes**

### Ingredients:

- 450 g top sirloin steaks, about 2 cm thick
- salt and pepper
- 2 large onions, thinly sliced
- 1 tablespoon extra-light olive oil
- 8 slider buns
- Horseradish Mayonnaise
- 1 cup light mayonnaise
- 4 teaspoons prepared horseradish
- 2 teaspoons Worcestershire sauce
- 1 teaspoon coarse brown mustard

### Directions:

1. Place steak in air fryer basket and cook at 200°C/390°F for 6 minutes. Turn and cook 6 more minutes for medium rare. If you prefer your steak medium, continue cooking for 3 minutes.
2. While the steak is cooking, prepare the Horseradish Mayonnaise by mixing all ingredients together.
3. When steak is cooked, remove from air fryer, sprinkle with salt and pepper to taste, and set aside to rest.
4. Toss the onion slices with the oil and place in air fryer basket. Cook at 200°C/390°F for 7 minutes, until onion rings are soft and browned.
5. Slice steak into very thin slices.
6. Spread slider buns with the horseradish mayo and pile on the meat and onions. Serve with remaining horseradish dressing for dipping.

### Variations & Ingredients Tips:

- Use Hawaiian rolls or mini pretzel buns instead of slider buns.
- Top with crumbled blue cheese or crispy fried onions.
- Serve with roasted garlic aioli or chimichurri sauce.

**Per Serving:** Calories: 406; Total Fat: 26g; Saturated Fat: 5g; Cholesterol: 57mg; Sodium: 515mg; Total Carbs: 23g; Dietary Fiber: 2g; Total Sugars: 5g; Protein: 22g

## Hot Avocado Fries

**Servings: 2 | Prep Time: 10 Minutes | Cooking Time: 20 Minutes**

### Ingredients:

- 1 egg
- 2 tbsp milk
- Salt and pepper to taste
- 1 cup crushed chili corn chips
- 2 tbsp Parmesan cheese
- 1 avocado, sliced into fries

### Directions:

1. Preheat air fryer at 190°C/375°F. In a bowl, beat egg and milk. In another bowl, add crushed chips, Parmesan cheese, salt and pepper. Dip avocado fries into the egg mixture, then dredge into crushed chips mixture to coat. Place avocado fries in the greased frying basket and Air Fry for 5 minutes. Serve immediately.

### Variations & Ingredients Tips:

- Use panko breadcrumbs or cornmeal instead of corn chips for the coating.
- Add some garlic powder, onion powder or smoked paprika to the breading.
- Serve with ranch dressing, salsa or guacamole for dipping.

**Per Serving:** Calories: 399; Total Fat: 29g; Saturated Fat: 6g; Cholesterol: 97mg; Sodium: 442mg; Total Carbs: 27g; Dietary Fiber: 7g; Total Sugars: 2g; Protein: 11g

## Spiced Nuts

**Servings: 3 | Prep Time: 10 Minutes | Cooking Time: 25 Minutes**

### Ingredients:

- 1 egg white, lightly beaten
- ¼ cup sugar
- 1 tsp salt
- ½ tsp ground cinnamon
- ¼ tsp ground cloves
- ¼ tsp ground allspice
- pinch ground cayenne pepper
- 1 cup pecan halves
- 1 cup cashews
- 1 cup almonds

### Directions:

1. Combine the egg white with the sugar and spices in a bowl. Preheat the air fryer to 150°C/300°F. Spray or brush the air fryer basket with vegetable oil. Toss the nuts together in the spiced egg white and transfer the nuts to the air fryer basket. Air-fry for 25 minutes, stirring the nuts in the basket a few times during the cooking process. Taste the nuts to see if they are crunchy and nicely toasted. Air-fry for a few more minutes if necessary. Serve warm or cool to room temperature and store in an airtight container for up to two weeks.

### Variations & Ingredients Tips:

- Use different types of nuts like walnuts, hazelnuts, or macadamia nuts for variety.
- Add dried fruit like raisins, cranberries, or apricots for a sweet and tangy twist.
- Experiment with different spice blends like pumpkin pie spice, curry powder, or Italian seasoning.

**Per Serving:** Calories: 715; Total Fat: 61g; Saturated Fat: 8g; Sodium: 783mg; Total Carbohydrates: 32g; Dietary Fiber: 10g; Total Sugars: 21g; Protein: 20g

## Prosciutto Polenta Rounds

**Servings: 6 | Prep Time: 15 Minutes | Cooking Time: 40 Minutes + 10 Minutes To Cool**

### Ingredients:

- 1 tube precooked polenta
- 1 tbsp garlic oil
- 115 g cream cheese, softened
- 3 tbsp mayonnaise
- 2 scallions, sliced
- 1 tbsp minced fresh chives
- 6 prosciutto slices, chopped

### Directions:

1. Preheat the air fryer to 200°C/400°F. Slice the polenta crosswise into 12 rounds. Brush both sides of each round with garlic oil and put 6 of them in the frying basket. Put a rack in the basket over the polenta and add the other 6 rounds. Bake for 15 minutes, flip, and cook for 10-15 more minutes or until the polenta is crispy and golden. While the polenta is cooking, beat the cream cheese and mayo and stir in the scallions, chives, and prosciutto. When the polenta is cooked, lay out on a wire rack to cool for 15 minutes. Top with the cream cheese mix and serve.

### Variations & Ingredients Tips:

- Use bacon, pancetta, or speck instead of prosciutto for a smoky flavor.
- Add grated Parmesan cheese, sun-dried tomatoes, or roasted garlic to the cream cheese mixture.
- Sprinkle with smoked paprika or cayenne pepper for a spicy kick.

**Per Serving:** Calories: 216; Total Fat: 15g; Saturated Fat: 6g; Cholesterol: 33mg; Sodium: 527mg; Total Carbs: 15g; Dietary Fiber: 1g; Total Sugars: 1g; Protein: 6g

## "Fried" Pickles With Homemade Ranch

**Servings: 8 | Prep Time: 15 Minutes | Cooking Time: 8 Minutes**

### Ingredients:

- 1 cup all-purpose flour
- 2 teaspoons dried dill
- ½ teaspoon paprika
- ¾ cup buttermilk
- 1 egg
- 4 large kosher dill pickles, sliced 6 mm thick
- 2 cups panko breadcrumbs

### Directions:

1. Preheat the air fryer to 190°C/380°F.
2. In a medium bowl, whisk together the flour, dill, paprika, buttermilk, and egg.
3. Dip and coat thick slices of dill pickles into the batter. Next, dredge into the panko breadcrumbs.
4. Place a single layer of breaded pickles into the air fryer basket. Spray the pickles with cooking spray. Cook for 4 minutes, turn over, and cook another 4 minutes. Repeat until all the pickle chips have been cooked.

### Variations & Ingredients Tips:

- Serve with your favorite ranch or blue cheese dressing for dipping.
- Try using zucchini or eggplant slices instead of pickles.
- Add some cayenne pepper or hot sauce to the batter for a spicy kick.

**Per Serving:** Calories: 216; Total Fat: 4g; Saturated Fat: 1g; Cholesterol: 27mg; Sodium: 689mg; Total Carbs: 36g; Dietary Fiber: 2g; Total Sugars: 4g; Protein: 7g

## Zucchini Fritters

**Servings: 8 | Prep Time: 15 Minutes | Cooking Time: 10 Minutes**

### Ingredients:

- 2 cups grated zucchini
- 1/2 teaspoon sea salt
- 1 egg
- 1/2 teaspoon garlic powder
- 1/4 teaspoon onion powder
- 1/4 cup grated Parmesan cheese
- 1/2 cup all-purpose flour
- 1/4 teaspoon baking powder
- 1/2 cup Greek yogurt or sour cream
- 1/2 lime, juiced
- 1/4 cup chopped cilantro
- 1/4 teaspoon ground cumin
- 1/4 teaspoon salt

### Directions:

1. Preheat the air fryer to 182°C/360°F.
2. In a large colander, place a kitchen towel. Inside the towel, place the grated zucchini and sprinkle the sea salt over the top. Let the zucchini sit for 5 minutes; then, using the towel, squeeze dry the zucchini.
3. In a medium bowl, mix together the egg, garlic powder, onion powder, Parmesan cheese, flour, and baking powder. Add in the grated zucchini, and stir until completely combined.
4. Pierce a piece of parchment paper with a fork 4 to 6 times. Place the parchment paper into the air fryer basket. Using a tablespoon, place 6 to 8 heaping tablespoons of fritter batter onto the parchment paper. Spray the fritters with cooking spray and cook for 5 minutes, turn the fritters over, and cook another 5 minutes.
5. Meanwhile, while the fritters are cooking, make the sauce. In a small bowl, whisk together the Greek yogurt or sour cream, lime juice, cilantro, cumin, and salt.
6. Repeat Steps 2–4 with the remaining batter.

### Variations & Ingredients Tips:

- Substitute panko breadcrumbs for some of the flour for a

crunchier texture.
- Add shredded cheddar or feta cheese to the batter for extra flavor.
- Use yellow summer squash or a mix of zucchini and squash for variety.

**Per Serving:** Calories: 305; Total Fat: 15g; Saturated Fat: 6g; Cholesterol: 111mg; Sodium: 1089mg; Total Carbs: 26g; Fiber: 4g; Sugars: 5g; Protein: 18g

## Fiery Cheese Sticks

**Servings: 4 | Prep Time: 10 Minutes | Cooking Time: 20 Minutes + Freezing Time**

### Ingredients:
- 1 egg, beaten
- ½ cup dried bread crumbs
- ¼ cup ground peanuts
- 1 tbsp chili powder
- ¼ tsp ground coriander
- ¼ tsp red pepper flakes
- ⅛ tsp cayenne pepper
- 8 mozzarella cheese sticks

### Directions:
1. Preheat the air fryer to 190°C/375°F. Beat the egg in a bowl, and on a plate, combine the breadcrumbs, peanuts, coriander, chili powder, pepper flakes, and cayenne. Dip each piece of string cheese in the egg, then in the breadcrumb mix. After lining a baking sheet with parchment paper, put the sticks on it and freeze them for 30 minutes. Get the sticks out of the freezer and set in the frying basket in a single layer. Spritz them with cooking oil. Air Fry for 7-9 minutes until the exterior is golden and the interior is hot and melted. Serve hot with marinara or ranch sauce.

### Variations & Ingredients Tips:
- Use panko breadcrumbs for a crunchier coating.
- Add some smoked paprika or garlic powder to the breading mixture.
- Serve with salsa, guacamole or queso dip for a Mexican twist.

**Per Serving:** Calories: 260; Total Fat: 15g; Saturated Fat: 7g; Cholesterol: 76mg; Sodium: 411mg; Total Carbs: 16g; Dietary Fiber: 2g; Total Sugars: 2g; Protein: 17g

## Asian-style Shrimp Toast

**Servings: 4 | Prep Time: 15 Minutes | Cooking Time: 25 Minutes**

### Ingredients:
- 8 large raw shrimp, chopped
- 1 egg white
- 2 garlic cloves, minced
- 1 red chili, minced
- 1 celery stalk, minced
- 2 tbsp cornstarch
- ¼ tsp Chinese five-spice
- 3 firm bread slices

### Directions:
1. Preheat air fryer to 175°C/350°F. Add the shrimp, egg white, garlic, red chili, celery, corn starch, and five-spice powder in a bowl and combine. Place 1/3 of the shrimp mix on a slice of bread, smearing it to the edges, then slice the bread into 4 strips. Lay the strips in the frying basket in a single layer and Air Fry for 3-6 minutes until golden and crispy. Repeat until all strips are cooked. Serve hot.

### Variations & Ingredients Tips:
- Use crabmeat instead of shrimp for a different flavor.
- Add some grated ginger to the shrimp mixture.
- Serve with a sweet chili sauce for dipping.

**Per Serving:** Calories: 130; Total Fat: 2g; Saturated Fat: 0g; Cholesterol: 49mg; Sodium: 319mg; Total Carbs: 19g; Dietary Fiber: 1g; Total Sugars: 2g; Protein: 9g

## Country Wings

**Servings: 4 | Prep Time: 10 Minutes | Cooking Time: 19 Minutes**

### Ingredients:
- 900 g chicken wings
- Marinade
- 1 cup buttermilk
- ½ teaspoon black pepper
- ½ teaspoon salt
- Coating
- 1 cup flour
- 1 cup panko breadcrumbs
- 2 teaspoons salt
- 2 tablespoons poultry seasoning
- oil for misting or cooking spray

### Directions:
1. Cut the tips off the wings. Discard or freeze for stock. Cut remaining wing sections apart at the joint to make 2 pieces per wing. Place wings in a large bowl or plastic bag.
2. Mix together all marinade ingredients and pour over wings. Refrigerate for at least 1 hour but for no more than 8 hours.
3. Preheat air fryer to 180°C/360°F.
4. Mix all coating ingredients together in a shallow dish or on wax paper.
5. Remove wings from marinade, shaking off excess, and roll in coating mixture.
6. Spray both sides of each wing with oil or cooking spray.
7. Place wings in air fryer basket in single layer, close but not too crowded. Cook for 19 minutes or until chicken is done and juices run clear.
8. Repeat step 7 to cook remaining wings.

### Variations & Ingredients Tips:
- Add some smoked paprika, cayenne pepper or hot sauce to the marinade for extra flavor.
- Use bone-in, skin-on chicken thighs instead of wings.
- Serve with ranch dressing, blue cheese dip or honey

mustard sauce.

**Per Serving:** Calories: 663; Total Fat: 34g; Saturated Fat: 10g; Cholesterol: 168mg; Sodium: 1738mg; Total Carbs: 45g; Dietary Fiber: 2g; Total Sugars: 5g; Protein: 44g

## Cheesy Zucchini Chips

**Servings: 4 | Prep Time: 20 Minutes | Cooking Time: 35 Minutes**

### Ingredients:

- 450 g thin zucchini chips
- 2 eggs
- ½ cup bread crumbs
- ½ cup grated Pecorino cheese
- Salt and pepper to taste
- ½ cup mayonnaise
- ½ tbsp olive oil
- ½ lemon. juiced
- 1 tsp garlic powder
- Salt and pepper to taste

### Directions:

1. Preheat air fryer to 175°C/350°F. Beat eggs in a small bowl, then set aside. In another small bowl, stir together bread crumbs, Pecorino, salt, and pepper. Dip zucchini slices into the egg mixture, then in the crumb mixture. Place them in the greased frying basket and Air Fry for 10 minutes. Remove and set aside to cool. Mix the mayonnaise, olive oil, lemon juice, garlic, salt, and pepper in a bowl to make aioli. Serve aioli with chips and enjoy.

### Variations & Ingredients Tips:

- Use yellow squash or eggplant slices instead of zucchini.
- Add some smoked paprika or Italian seasoning to the breadcrumb mixture.
- Serve with marinara sauce or ranch dressing for dipping.

**Per Serving:** Calories: 313; Total Fat: 24g; Saturated Fat: 6g; Cholesterol: 111mg; Sodium: 513mg; Total Carbs: 15g; Dietary Fiber: 2g; Total Sugars: 4g; Protein: 11g

## Crab Toasts

**Servings: 15 | Prep Time: 10 Minutes | Cooking Time: 5 Minutes**

### Ingredients:

- 1 170 g can flaked crabmeat, well drained
- 3 tablespoons light mayonnaise
- ½ teaspoon lemon juice
- 1 teaspoon Worcestershire sauce
- ¼ cup shredded sharp Cheddar cheese
- ¼ cup shredded Parmesan cheese
- 1 loaf artisan bread, French bread, or baguette, cut into slices 10 mm thick

### Directions:

1. Mix together all ingredients except the bread slices.
2. Spread each slice of bread with a thin layer of crabmeat mixture. (For a bread slice measuring 5 x 4 cm you will need about ½ tablespoon of crab mixture.)
3. Place in air fryer basket in single layer and cook at 180°C/360°F for 5 minutes or until tops brown and toast is crispy.
4. Repeat step 3 to cook remaining crab toasts.

### Variations & Ingredients Tips:

- Use smoked salmon, cooked shrimp or lobster instead of crab.
- Add some minced jalapeños or hot sauce to the mixture for a spicy kick.
- Sprinkle with Old Bay seasoning or smoked paprika before cooking.

**Per Serving:** Calories: 104; Total Fat: 4g; Saturated Fat: 1g; Cholesterol: 17mg; Sodium: 271mg; Total Carbs: 12g; Dietary Fiber: 1g; Total Sugars: 1g; Protein: 5g

## Artichoke-spinach Dip

**Servings: 4 | Prep Time: 10 Minutes | Cooking Time: 25 Minutes**

### Ingredients:

- 113 g canned artichoke hearts, chopped
- ½ cup Greek yogurt
- ¼ cup cream cheese
- ½ cup spinach, chopped
- ½ red bell pepper, chopped
- 1 garlic clove, minced
- ½ tsp dried oregano
- 3 tsp grated Parmesan cheese

### Directions:

1. Preheat air fryer to 170°C/340°F. Mix the yogurt and cream cheese. Add the artichoke, spinach, red bell pepper, garlic, and oregano, then put the mix in a pan and scatter Parmesan cheese on top. Put the pan in the frying basket and Bake for 9-14 minutes. The dip should be bubbly and brown. Serve hot.

### Variations & Ingredients Tips:

- Add some jalapeños or red pepper flakes for a spicy kick.
- Top with shredded mozzarella before cooking for extra cheesiness.
- Serve with sliced baguette, pita chips or fresh vegetables for dipping.

**Per Serving:** Calories: 126; Total Fat: 9g; Saturated Fat: 5g; Cholesterol: 19mg; Sodium: 288mg; Total Carbs: 7g; Dietary Fiber: 2g; Total Sugars: 3g; Protein: 6g

## Avocado Fries With Quick Salsa Fresca

**Servings: 4 | Prep Time: 20 Minutes | Cooking Time:**

**6 Minutes**

### Ingredients:

- ½ cup flour
- 2 teaspoons salt
- 2 eggs, lightly beaten
- 1 cup panko breadcrumbs*
- ⅛ teaspoon cayenne pepper
- ¼ teaspoon smoked paprika (optional)
- 2 large avocados, just ripe
- vegetable oil, in a spray bottle
- Quick Salsa Fresca
- 1 cup cherry tomatoes
- 1 2.5 cm chunk of shallot or red onion
- 2 teaspoons fresh lime juice
- 1 teaspoon chopped fresh cilantro or parsley
- salt and freshly ground black pepper

### Directions:

1. Set up a dredging station with three shallow dishes. Place the flour and salt in the first shallow dish. Place the eggs into the second dish. Combine the breadcrumbs, cayenne pepper and paprika (if using) in the third dish.
2. Preheat the air fryer to 200°C/400°F.
3. Cut the avocado in half around the pit and separate the two sides. Slice the avocados into long strips while still in their skin. Run a spoon around the slices, separating them from the avocado skin. Try to keep the slices whole, but don't worry if they break – you can still coat and air-fry the pieces.
4. Coat the avocado slices by dredging them first in the flour, then the egg and then the breadcrumbs, pressing the crumbs on gently with your hands. Set the coated avocado fries on a tray and spray them on all sides with vegetable oil.
5. Air-fry the avocado fries, one layer at a time, at 200°C/400°F for 6 minutes, turning them over halfway through the cooking time and spraying lightly again if necessary. When the fries are nicely browned on all sides, season with salt and remove.
6. While the avocado fries are air-frying, make the salsa fresca by combining everything in a food processor. Pulse several times until the salsa is a chunky purée. Serve the fries warm with the salsa on the side for dipping.

### Variations & Ingredients Tips:

- Use plantains instead of avocados for a Caribbean twist.
- Add some grated Parmesan to the breadcrumb mixture.
- Serve with a creamy cilantro-lime dipping sauce.

**Per Serving:** Calories: 401; Total Fat: 27g; Saturated Fat: 5g; Cholesterol: 93mg; Sodium: 1188mg; Total Carbs: 35g; Dietary Fiber: 9g; Total Sugars: 4g; Protein: 9g

## Greek Street Tacos

**Servings: 8 | Prep Time: 10 Minutes | Cooking Time: 3 Minutes**

### Ingredients:

- 8 small flour tortillas (10 cm diameter)
- 8 tablespoons hummus
- 4 tablespoons crumbled feta cheese
- 4 tablespoons chopped kalamata or other olives (optional)
- olive oil for misting

### Directions:

1. Place 1 tablespoon of hummus or tapenade in the center of each tortilla. Top with 1 teaspoon of feta crumbles and 1 teaspoon of chopped olives, if using.
2. Using your finger or a small spoon, moisten the edges of the tortilla all around with water.
3. Fold tortilla over to make a half-moon shape. Press center gently. Then press the edges firmly to seal in the filling.
4. Mist both sides with olive oil.
5. Place in air fryer basket very close but try not to overlap.
6. Cook at 200°C/390°F for 3 minutes, just until lightly browned and crispy.

### Variations & Ingredients Tips:

- Use pita bread, naan or flatbread instead of tortillas.
- Add some diced tomatoes, cucumbers or red onions to the filling.
- Drizzle with tzatziki sauce, balsamic glaze or hot sauce before serving.

**Per Serving:** Calories: 125; Total Fat: 5g; Saturated Fat: 1g; Cholesterol: 6mg; Sodium: 263mg; Total Carbs: 17g; Dietary Fiber: 1g; Total Sugars: 0g; Protein: 4g

## Polenta Fries With Chili-lime Mayo

**Servings: 4 | Prep Time: 10 Minutes | Cooking Time: 28 Minutes**

### Ingredients:

- 2 tsp vegetable or olive oil
- ¼ tsp paprika
- 450 g prepared polenta, cut into 8-cm x 1.3-cm sticks
- salt and freshly ground black pepper
- Chili-Lime Mayo
- ½ cup mayonnaise
- 1 tsp chili powder
- ¼ tsp ground cumin
- juice of half a lime
- 1 tsp chopped fresh cilantro
- salt and freshly ground black pepper

### Directions:

1. Preheat the air fryer to 200°C/400°F. Combine the oil and paprika and then carefully toss the polenta sticks in the mixture. Air-fry the polenta fries at 200°C/400°F for 15 minutes. Gently shake the basket to rotate the fries and continue to air-fry for another 13 minutes or until the fries have browned nicely. Season to taste with salt and freshly ground black pepper. To make the chili-lime mayo, com-

bine all the ingredients in a small bowl and stir well. Serve the polenta fries warm with chili-lime mayo on the side for dipping.

**Variations & Ingredients Tips:**

- Add grated Parmesan cheese or finely chopped herbs to the polenta mixture before frying.
- Serve with different dipping sauces like garlic aioli, marinara, or ranch dressing.
- For a spicier version, add cayenne pepper or red pepper flakes to the polenta mixture.

**Per Serving:** Calories: 286; Total Fat: 22g; Saturated Fat: 3g; Cholesterol: 12mg; Sodium: 486mg; Total Carbs: 20g; Dietary Fiber: 2g; Total Sugars: 0g; Protein: 2g

## Parmesan Pizza Nuggets

**Servings: 8 | Prep Time: 20 Minutes | Cooking Time: 6 Minutes**

### Ingredients:

- ¾ cup warm filtered water
- 1 package fast-rising yeast
- ½ tsp salt
- 2 cups all-purpose flour
- ¼ cup finely grated Parmesan cheese
- 1 tsp Italian seasoning
- 2 tbsp extra-virgin olive oil
- 1 tsp kosher salt

### Directions:

1. Preheat the air fryer to 190°C/370°F. In a large microwave-safe bowl, add the water. Heat for 40 seconds in the microwave. Remove and mix in the yeast and salt. Let sit 5 minutes. Meanwhile, in a medium bowl, mix the flour with the Parmesan cheese and Italian seasoning. Set aside. Using a stand mixer with a dough hook attachment, add the yeast liquid and then mix in the flour mixture ⅓ cup at a time until all the flour mixture is added and a dough is formed. Remove the bowl from the stand, and then let the dough rise for 1 hour in a warm space, covered with a kitchen towel. After the dough has doubled in size, remove it from the bowl and punch it down a few times on a lightly floured flat surface. Divide the dough into 4 balls, and then roll each ball out into a long, skinny, sticklike shape. Using a sharp knife, cut each dough stick into 6 pieces. Repeat for the remaining dough balls until you have about 24 nuggets formed. Lightly brush the top of each bite with the egg whites and cover with a pinch of sea salt. Spray the air fryer basket with olive oil spray and place the pizza nuggets on top. Cook for 6 minutes, or until lightly browned. Remove and keep warm. Repeat until all the nuggets are cooked. Serve warm.

**Variations & Ingredients Tips:**

- Add finely chopped pepperoni, sausage, or veggies to the dough for a stuffed pizza nugget.
- Serve with warm marinara sauce or ranch dressing for dipping.
- Sprinkle with additional grated Parmesan cheese or Italian seasoning before serving.

**Per Serving:** Calories: 157; Total Fat: 5g; Saturated Fat: 1g; Cholesterol: 1mg; Sodium: 372mg; Total Carbs: 24g; Dietary Fiber: 1g; Total Sugars: 0g; Protein: 5g

# Poultry Recipes

## Chicken Breasts Wrapped In Bacon

**Servings: 4 | Prep Time: 10 Minutes | Cooking Time: 35 Minutes**

### Ingredients:

- ¼ cup mayonnaise
- ¼ cup sour cream
- 3 tbsp ketchup
- 1 tbsp yellow mustard
- 1 tbsp light brown sugar
- 454 grams chicken tenders
- 1 tsp dried parsley
- 8 bacon slices

### Directions:

1. Preheat the air fryer to 190°C/370°F.
2. Combine the mayonnaise, sour cream, ketchup, mustard, and brown sugar in a bowl and mix well, then set aside.
3. Sprinkle the chicken with the parsley and wrap each one in a slice of bacon.
4. Put the wrapped chicken in the air fryer basket in a single layer and Air Fry for 18-20 minutes, flipping once until the bacon is crisp.
5. Serve with sauce.

**Variations & Ingredients Tips:**

- Substitute bacon with prosciutto or pancetta for a different smoky flavor.

- Brush the wrapped chicken with BBQ sauce, teriyaki sauce, or honey mustard before air frying.
- Serve with a side of roasted vegetables or sweet potato fries.

**Per Serving:** Calories: 470; Total Fat: 35g; Saturated Fat: 9g; Sodium: 940mg; Total Carbohydrates: 8g; Dietary Fiber: 0g; Total Sugars: 7g; Protein: 33g

## Chicken Salad With Roasted Vegetables

**Servings: 4 | Prep Time: 10 Minutes | Cooking Time: 25 Minutes**

### Ingredients:

- 4 tbsp honey-mustard salad dressing
- 3 chicken breasts, cubed
- 1 red onion, sliced
- 1 orange bell pepper, sliced
- 1 cup sliced zucchini
- ½ tsp dried thyme
- ½ cup mayonnaise
- 2 tbsp lemon juice

### Directions:

1. Preheat air fryer to 200°C/400°F.
2. Add chicken, onion, pepper, and zucchini to the fryer. Drizzle with 1 tbsp of the salad dressing and sprinkle with thyme. Toss to coat.
3. Bake for 5-6 minutes. Shake the basket, then continue cooking for another 5-6 minutes.
4. In a bowl, combine the rest of the dressing, mayonnaise, and lemon juice.
5. Transfer the chicken and vegetables and toss to coat.
6. Serve and enjoy!

### Variations & Ingredients Tips:

- Use a different dressing like ranch, Italian, or balsamic vinaigrette.
- Add cherry tomatoes, mushrooms, or eggplant to the vegetable mix.
- Serve over a bed of mixed greens or spinach for extra nutrients.

**Per Serving:** Calories: 420; Total Fat: 28g; Saturated Fat: 5g; Sodium: 420mg; Total Carbohydrates: 11g; Dietary Fiber: 2g; Total Sugars: 7g; Protein: 32g

## Chicken Meatballs With A Surprise

**Servings: 4 | Prep Time: 15 Minutes | Cooking Time: 35 Minutes**

### Ingredients:

- 1/3 cup cottage cheese crumbles
- 450g ground chicken
- 1/2 tsp onion powder
- 1/4 cup chopped basil
- 1/2 cup bread crumbs
- 1/2 tsp garlic powder

### Directions:

1. Preheat air fryer to 175°C/350°F.
2. Combine the ground chicken, onion powder, basil, cottage cheese, bread crumbs, and garlic powder in a bowl.
3. Form into 18 meatballs, about 2 tbsp each.
4. Place the chicken meatballs in the greased frying basket and Air Fry for 12 minutes, shaking once.
5. Serve.

### Variations & Ingredients Tips:

- Use ground turkey instead of chicken.
- Add grated parmesan or shredded mozzarella cheese.
- Serve meatballs with marinara sauce for dipping.

**Per Serving (4-5 meatballs):** Calories: 230; Total Fat: 8g; Saturated Fat: 2g; Cholesterol: 106mg; Sodium: 384mg; Total Carbs: 14g; Dietary Fiber: 1g; Total Sugars: 1g; Protein: 25g

## Chicken Pigs In Blankets

**Servings: 4 | Prep Time: 10 Minutes | Cooking Time: 40 Minutes**

### Ingredients:

- 8 chicken drumsticks, boneless, skinless
- 2 tbsp light brown sugar
- 2 tbsp ketchup
- 1 tbsp grainy mustard
- 8 smoked bacon slices
- 1 tsp chopped fresh sage

### Directions:

1. Preheat the air fryer to 175°C/350°F.
2. Mix brown sugar, sage, ketchup, and mustard in a bowl and brush the chicken with it.
3. Wrap slices of bacon around the drumsticks and brush with the remaining mix.
4. Line the frying basket with round parchment paper with holes.
5. Set 4 drumsticks on the paper, add a raised rack and set the other drumsticks on it.
6. Bake for 25-35 minutes, moving the bottom drumsticks to the top, top to the bottom, and flipping at about 14-16 minutes.
7. Sprinkle with sage and serve.

### Variations & Ingredients Tips:

- Use chicken thighs instead of drumsticks.
- Add a touch of hot sauce to the glaze for some heat.
- Wrap turkey bacon instead of pork bacon for a leaner option.

**Per Serving (2 pigs in blankets):** Calories: 296; Total Fat: 11g; Saturated Fat: 4g; Cholesterol: 114mg; Sodium: 832mg; Total Carbs: 18g; Dietary Fiber: 1g; Total Sugars: 10g; Protein: 31g

## Thai Turkey And Zucchini Meatballs

**Servings: 4 | Prep Time: 15 Minutes | Cooking Time: 12 Minutes**

### Ingredients:

- 1 1/2 cups grated zucchini, squeezed dry (about 1 large zucchini)
- 3 scallions, finely chopped
- 2 cloves garlic, minced
- 1 tablespoon grated fresh ginger
- 1 tablespoon finely chopped fresh cilantro
- Zest of 1 lime
- 1 teaspoon salt
- Freshly ground black pepper
- 680g ground turkey
- 2 eggs, lightly beaten
- 1 cup Thai sweet chili sauce
- Lime wedges, for serving

### Directions:

1. Mix zucchini, scallions, garlic, ginger, cilantro, lime zest, salt, pepper, turkey and eggs.
2. Form into 24 golfball-sized meatballs.
3. Preheat air fryer to 195°C/380°F.
4. Air fry meatballs in batches for 12 mins, turning halfway.
5. Toss cooked meatballs in sweet chili sauce.
6. Serve over noodles/rice with extra sauce and lime wedges.

### Variations & Ingredients Tips:

- Use ground chicken instead of turkey.
- Add shredded carrots or water chestnuts to the meatball mixture.
- Bake meatballs in oven at 400°F for 15-18 mins if no air fryer.

**Per Serving (6 meatballs):** Calories: 349; Total Fat: 14g; Saturated Fat: 3g; Cholesterol: 181mg; Sodium: 979mg; Total Carbs: 22g; Dietary Fiber: 1g; Total Sugars: 15g; Protein: 34g

## Chicago-style Turkey Meatballs

**Servings: 6 | Prep Time: 10 Minutes | Cooking Time: 15 Minutes**

### Ingredients:

- 454 grams ground turkey
- 1 tbsp orange juice
- Salt and pepper to taste
- ½ tsp smoked paprika
- ½ tsp chili powder
- 1 tsp cumin powder
- ¼ red bell pepper, diced
- 1 diced jalapeño pepper
- 2 garlic cloves, minced

### Directions:

1. Preheat air fryer to 200°C/400°F.
2. Combine all of the ingredients in a large bowl. Shape into meatballs.
3. Transfer the meatballs into the greased air fryer basket.
4. Air Fry for 4 minutes, then flip the meatballs. Air Fry for another 3 minutes until cooked through.
5. Serve immediately.

### Variations & Ingredients Tips:

- Use ground chicken, beef, or pork instead of turkey.
- Add grated Parmesan cheese or breadcrumbs to the mixture for a different texture.
- Serve with marinara sauce, BBQ sauce, or ranch dressing for dipping.

**Per Serving:** Calories: 170; Total Fat: 10g; Saturated Fat: 3g; Sodium: 120mg; Total Carbohydrates: 2g; Dietary Fiber: 0g; Total Sugars: 1g; Protein: 18g

## Chicken Skewers

**Servings: 4 | Prep Time: 20 Minutes | Cooking Time: 55 Minutes**

### Ingredients:

- 454 grams boneless skinless chicken thighs, cut into pieces
- 1 sweet onion, cut into 2.5-cm pieces
- 1 zucchini, cut into 2.5-cm pieces
- 1 red bell pepper, cut into 2.5-cm pieces
- ¼ cup olive oil
- 1 tsp garlic powder
- 1 tsp shallot powder
- 1 tsp ground cumin
- ½ tsp dried oregano
- ½ tsp dried thyme
- ¼ cup lemon juice
- 1 tbsp apple cider vinegar
- 12 grape tomatoes

### Directions:

1. Combine the olive oil, garlic powder, shallot powder, cumin, oregano, thyme, lemon juice, and vinegar in a bowl; mix well. Alternate skewering the chicken, bell pepper, onion, zucchini, and tomatoes. Once all of the skewers are prepared, place them in a greased baking dish and pour the olive oil marinade over the top. Turn to coat. Cover with plastic wrap and refrigerate.
2. Preheat air fryer to 190°C/380°F.
3. Remove the skewers from the marinade and arrange them in a single layer on the air fryer basket. Bake for 25 minutes, rotating once. Let the skewers sit for 5 minutes.
4. Serve and enjoy!

### Variations & Ingredients Tips:

- Use pork, beef, or shrimp instead of chicken for different protein options.
- Add mushrooms, eggplant, or yellow squash to the skewers for more veggies.
- Brush with BBQ sauce, teriyaki sauce, or pesto during the last few minutes of cooking.

**Per Serving:** Calories: 330; Total Fat: 20g; Saturated Fat: 3.5g; Sodium: 110mg; Total Carbohydrates: 9g; Dietary Fiber:

3g; Total Sugars: 5g; Protein: 29g

## Chicken Souvlaki Gyros

**Servings: 4 | Prep Time: 15 Minutes (plus 2 Hours Marinating Time) | Cooking Time: 18 Minutes**

### Ingredients:

- ¼ cup extra-virgin olive oil
- 1 clove garlic, crushed
- 1 tablespoon Italian seasoning
- ½ teaspoon paprika
- ½ lemon, sliced
- ¼ teaspoon salt
- 454 grams boneless, skinless chicken breasts
- 4 whole-grain pita breads
- 1 cup shredded lettuce
- ½ cup chopped tomatoes
- ¼ cup chopped red onion
- ¼ cup cucumber yogurt sauce

### Directions:

1. In a large resealable plastic bag, combine the olive oil, garlic, Italian seasoning, paprika, lemon, and salt. Add the chicken to the bag and secure shut. Vigorously shake until all the ingredients are combined. Set in the fridge for 2 hours to marinate.
2. When ready to cook, preheat the air fryer to 180°C/360°F.
3. Liberally spray the air fryer basket with olive oil mist. Remove the chicken from the bag and discard the leftover marinade. Place the chicken into the air fryer basket, allowing enough room between the chicken breasts to flip.
4. Cook for 10 minutes, flip, and cook another 8 minutes.
5. Remove the chicken from the air fryer basket when it has cooked (or the internal temperature of the chicken reaches 74°C/165°F). Let rest 5 minutes. Then thinly slice the chicken into strips.
6. Assemble the gyros by placing the pita bread on a flat surface and topping with chicken, lettuce, tomatoes, onion, and a drizzle of yogurt sauce.
7. Serve warm.

### Variations & Ingredients Tips:

- Use Greek seasoning or za'atar spice blend instead of Italian seasoning.
- Add crumbled feta cheese or sliced Kalamata olives as toppings.
- Serve with a side of Greek salad or lemon-roasted potatoes.

**Per Serving:** Calories: 430; Total Fat: 19g; Saturated Fat: 3g; Sodium: 480mg; Total Carbohydrates: 30g; Dietary Fiber: 5g; Total Sugars: 4g; Protein: 37g

## Fennel & Chicken Ratatouille

**Servings: 4 | Prep Time: 20 Minutes | Cooking Time: 30 Minutes**

### Ingredients:

- 450g boneless, skinless chicken thighs, cubed
- 2 tbsp grated Parmesan cheese
- 1 eggplant, cubed
- 1 zucchini, cubed
- 1 bell pepper, diced
- 1 fennel bulb, sliced
- 1 tsp salt
- 1 tsp Italian seasoning
- 2 tbsp olive oil
- 1 can (400g) diced tomatoes
- 1 tsp pasta sauce
- 2 tbsp basil leaves

### Directions:

1. Preheat air fryer to 200°C/400°F.
2. Mix the chicken, eggplant, zucchini, bell pepper, fennel, salt, Italian seasoning, and oil in a bowl.
3. Place the chicken mixture in the frying basket and Air Fry for 7 minutes. Transfer it to a cake pan.
4. Mix in tomatoes along with juices and pasta sauce. Air Fry for 8 minutes.
5. Scatter with Parmesan and basil. Serve.

### Variations & Ingredients Tips:

- Use other vegetables like mushrooms, onions or summer squash.
- Substitute fennel with celery for a milder flavor.
- Serve over pasta, rice or with crusty bread.

**Per Serving:** Calories: 320; Total Fat: 17g; Saturated Fat: 4g; Cholesterol: 105mg; Sodium: 820mg; Total Carbs: 16g; Dietary Fiber: 5g; Total Sugars: 8g; Protein: 27g

## Favorite Fried Chicken Wings

**Servings: 4 | Prep Time: 15 Minutes | Cooking Time: 30 Minutes**

### Ingredients:

- 16 chicken wings
- 1 tsp garlic powder
- 1/2 tsp paprika
- 1 tsp chicken seasoning
- Black pepper to taste
- 1/2 cup flour
- 1/4 cup sour cream
- 2 tsp red chili flakes

### Directions:

1. Preheat air fryer to 200°C/400°F.
2. Put the drumettes in a resealable bag along with garlic powder, chicken seasoning, paprika, and pepper. Seal the bag and shake until the chicken is completely coated.
3. Prepare a clean resealable bag and add the flour. Pour sour cream in a large bowl.
4. Dunk the drumettes into the sour cream, then transfer them to the bag of flour. Seal the bag and shake until coated and repeat until all of the wings are coated.
5. Transfer the drumettes to the frying basket. Lightly spray them with cooking oil and Air Fry for 23-25 minutes, shaking the basket a few times until crispy and golden brown.
6. Allow to cool slightly. Sprinkle with red chili flakes and

serve.

### Variations & Ingredients Tips:

- Toss the cooked wings in your favorite wing sauce like Buffalo or BBQ.
- Marinate the wings overnight in buttermilk for extra tenderness.
- Serve with celery sticks and blue cheese dressing.

**Per Serving:** Calories: 470; Total Fat: 32g; Saturated Fat: 10g; Cholesterol: 155mg; Sodium: 620mg; Total Carbs: 14g; Dietary Fiber: 1g; Total Sugars: 1g; Protein: 33g

## Coconut Chicken With Apricot-ginger Sauce

**Servings: 4 | Prep Time: 20 Minutes | Cooking Time: 8 Minutes Per Batch**

### Ingredients:

- 680 grams boneless, skinless chicken tenders, cut in large chunks (about 3 cm)
- salt and pepper
- ½ cup cornstarch
- 2 eggs
- 1 tablespoon milk
- 3 cups shredded coconut (see below)
- oil for misting or cooking spray
- Apricot-Ginger Sauce
- ½ cup apricot preserves
- 2 tablespoons white vinegar
- ¼ teaspoon ground ginger
- ¼ teaspoon low-sodium soy sauce
- 2 teaspoons white or yellow onion, grated or finely minced

### Directions:

1. Mix all ingredients for the Apricot-Ginger Sauce well and let sit for flavors to blend while you cook the chicken.
2. Season chicken chunks with salt and pepper to taste.
3. Place cornstarch in a shallow dish.
4. In another shallow dish, beat together eggs and milk.
5. Place coconut in a third shallow dish. (If also using panko breadcrumbs, as suggested below, stir them to mix well.)
6. Spray air fryer basket with oil or cooking spray.
7. Dip each chicken chunk into cornstarch, shake off excess, and dip in egg mixture.
8. Shake off excess egg mixture and roll lightly in coconut or coconut mixture. Spray with oil.
9. Place coated chicken chunks in air fryer basket in a single layer, close together but without sides touching.
10. Cook at 180°C/360°F for 4 minutes, stop, and turn chunks over.
11. Cook an additional 4 minutes or until chicken is done inside and coating is crispy brown.
12. Repeat steps 9 through 11 to cook remaining chicken chunks.

### Variations & Ingredients Tips:

- Substitute apricot preserves with peach, mango, or pineapple for different fruity sauces.
- Add a pinch of cayenne pepper or red pepper flakes to the sauce for a spicy kick.
- Mix shredded coconut with panko breadcrumbs for an extra crispy coating.

**Per Serving:** Calories: 610; Total Fat: 29g; Saturated Fat: 20g; Sodium: 430mg; Total Carbohydrates: 52g; Dietary Fiber: 5g; Total Sugars: 29g; Protein: 39g

## Philly Chicken Cheesesteak Stromboli

**Servings: 2 | Prep Time: 30 Minutes | Cooking Time: 28 Minutes**

### Ingredients:

- ½ onion, sliced
- 1 teaspoon vegetable oil
- 2 boneless, skinless chicken breasts, partially frozen and sliced very thin on the bias (about 450g)
- 1 tablespoon Worcestershire sauce
- Salt and freshly ground black pepper
- ½ recipe of Blue Jean
- Chef pizza dough, or 400g of store-bought pizza dough
- 1½ cups grated Cheddar cheese
- ½ cup Cheese Whiz® (or other jarred cheese sauce), warmed gently in the microwave
- Tomato ketchup for serving

### Directions:

1. Preheat the air fryer to 200°C/400°F.
2. Toss the sliced onion with oil and air-fry for 8 minutes, stirring halfway through the cooking time. Add the sliced chicken and Worcestershire sauce to the air fryer basket, and toss to evenly distribute the ingredients. Season the mixture with salt and freshly ground black pepper and air-fry for 8 minutes, stirring a couple of times during the cooking process. Remove the chicken and onion from the air fryer and let the mixture cool a little.
3. On a lightly floured surface, roll or press the pizza dough out into a 33-cm by 28-cm rectangle, with the long side closest to you. Sprinkle half of the Cheddar cheese over the dough leaving an empty 2.5-cm border from the edge farthest away from you. Top the cheese with the chicken and onion mixture, spreading it out evenly. Drizzle the cheese sauce over the meat and sprinkle the remaining Cheddar cheese on top.
4. Start rolling the stromboli away from you and toward the empty border. Make sure the filling stays tightly tucked inside the roll. Finally, tuck the ends of the dough in and pinch the seam shut. Place the seam side down and shape the Stromboli into a U-shape to fit in the air-fry basket. Cut 4 small slits with the tip of a sharp knife evenly in the top of the dough and lightly brush the stromboli with a little

oil.
5. Preheat the air fryer to 190°C/370°F.
6. Spray or brush the air fryer basket with oil and transfer the U-shaped stromboli to the air fryer basket. Air-fry for 12 minutes, turning the stromboli over halfway through the cooking time. (Use a plate to invert the stromboli out of the air fryer basket and then slide it back into the basket off the plate.)
7. To remove, carefully flip stromboli over onto a cutting board. Let it rest for a couple of minutes before serving. Slice the stromboli into 5-cm pieces and serve with ketchup for dipping, if desired.

### Variations & Ingredients Tips:

- Use thinly sliced roast beef instead of chicken for a classic Philly cheesesteak.
- Add sautéed bell peppers and mushrooms to the filling.
- Brush the stromboli with garlic butter before air frying for extra flavor.

**Per Serving:** Calories: 970; Total Fat: 51g; Saturated Fat: 24g; Cholesterol: 210mg; Sodium: 1740mg; Total Carbs: 61g; Dietary Fiber: 3g; Total Sugars: 6g; Protein: 72g

## German Chicken Frikadellen

**Servings: 6 | Prep Time: 10 Minutes | Cooking Time: 20 Minutes**

### Ingredients:

- 450g ground chicken
- 1 egg
- 3/4 cup bread crumbs
- 1/4 cup diced onions
- 1 grated carrot
- 1 tsp yellow mustard
- Salt and pepper to taste
- 1/4 cup chopped parsley

### Directions:

1. Preheat air fryer at 175°C/350°F.
2. In a bowl, combine the ground chicken, egg, crumbs, onions, carrot, parsley, salt, and pepper. Mix well with your hands.
3. Form mixture into meatballs. Place them in the frying basket and Air Fry for 8-10 minutes, tossing once until golden.
4. Serve right away.

### Variations & Ingredients Tips:

- Substitute half the ground chicken with ground pork for a more traditional flavor.
- Add some paprika or cayenne pepper for a spicy kick.
- Serve with sauerkraut and mustard on the side.

**Per Serving:** Calories: 210; Total Fat: 10g; Saturated Fat: 3g; Cholesterol: 110mg; Sodium: 200mg; Total Carbs: 11g; Dietary Fiber: 1g; Total Sugars: 2g; Protein: 19g

## Spinach & Turkey Meatballs

**Servings: 4 | Prep Time: 10 Minutes | Cooking Time: 45 Minutes**

### Ingredients:

- 1/4 cup grated Parmesan cheese
- 2 scallions, chopped
- 1 garlic clove, minced
- 1 egg, beaten
- 1 cup baby spinach
- 1/4 cup bread crumbs
- 1 tsp dried oregano
- Salt and pepper to taste
- 565g ground turkey

### Directions:

1. Preheat the air fryer to 205°C/400°F and preheat the oven to 120°C/250°F.
2. Combine the scallions, garlic, egg, baby spinach, breadcrumbs, Parmesan, oregano, salt, and pepper in a bowl and mix well.
3. Add the turkey and mix, then form into 3.8cm meatballs.
4. Add as many meatballs as will fit in a single layer in the frying basket and Air Fry for 10-15 minutes, shaking once around minute 7.
5. Put the cooked meatballs on a tray in the oven and cover with foil to keep warm. Repeat with the remaining balls.

### Variations & Ingredients Tips:

- Add breadcrumbs if mixture seems too wet to form balls.
- Use ground chicken or beef instead of turkey.
- Serve meatballs with marinara sauce for dipping.

**Per Serving (6 meatballs):** Calories: 268; Total Fat: 13g; Saturated Fat: 4g; Cholesterol: 136mg; Sodium: 455mg; Total Carbs: 10g; Dietary Fiber: 1g; Total Sugars: 1g; Protein: 28g

## Spicy Black Bean Turkey Burgers With Cumin-avocado Spread

**Servings: 2 | Prep Time: 10 Minutes | Cooking Time: 20 Minutes**

### Ingredients:

- 1 cup canned black beans, drained and rinsed
- 340g lean ground turkey
- 2 tablespoons minced red onion
- 1 Jalapeño pepper, seeded and minced
- 2 tablespoons plain breadcrumbs
- 1/2 teaspoon chili powder
- 1/4 teaspoon cayenne pepper
- Salt, to taste
- Olive or vegetable oil
- 2 slices pepper jack cheese
- Toasted burger rolls, sliced tomatoes, lettuce leaves
- Cumin-Avocado Spread:
- 1 ripe avocado
- Juice of 1 lime
- 1 teaspoon ground cumin
- 1/2 teaspoon salt
- 1 tablespoon chopped

- fresh cilantro
- Freshly ground black pepper

### Directions:

1. Place the black beans in a large bowl and smash them slightly with the back of a fork. Add the ground turkey, red onion, Jalapeño pepper, breadcrumbs, chili powder and cayenne pepper. Season with salt. Mix with your hands to combine all the ingredients and then shape them into 2 patties. Brush both sides of the burger patties with a little olive or vegetable oil.
2. Preheat the air fryer to 190°C/380°F.
3. Transfer the burgers to the air fryer basket and air-fry for 20 minutes, flipping them over halfway through the cooking process. Top the burgers with the pepper jack cheese (securing the slices to the burgers with a toothpick) for the last 2 minutes of the cooking process.
4. While the burgers are cooking, make the cumin avocado spread. Place the avocado, lime juice, cumin and salt in food processor and process until smooth. (For a chunkier spread, you can mash this by hand in a bowl.) Stir in the cilantro and season with freshly ground black pepper. Chill the spread until you are ready to serve.
5. When the burgers have finished cooking, remove them from the air fryer and let them rest on a plate, covered gently with aluminum foil. Brush a little olive oil on the insides of the burger rolls. Place the rolls, cut side up, into the air fryer basket and air-fry at 200°C/400°F for 1 minute to toast and warm them.
6. Spread the cumin-avocado spread on the rolls and build your burgers with lettuce and sliced tomatoes and any other ingredient you like. Serve warm with a side of sweet potato fries.

### Variations & Ingredients Tips:

- Use black bean veggie patties instead of turkey for a vegetarian option.
- Add crumbled feta or shredded cheddar to the burger patty mixture.
- Serve on whole wheat buns or lettuce wraps.

**Per Serving (1 burger + spread):** Calories: 566; Total Fat: 24g; Saturated Fat: 6g; Cholesterol: 115mg; Sodium: 647mg; Total Carbs: 46g; Dietary Fiber: 14g; Total Sugars: 4g; Protein: 43g

## Southern-fried Chicken Livers

**Servings: 4 | Prep Time: 20 Minutes | Cooking Time: 12 Minutes**

### Ingredients:

- 2 eggs
- 2 tablespoons water
- ¾ cup flour
- 1½ cups panko breadcrumbs
- ½ cup plain breadcrumbs
- 1 teaspoon salt
- ½ teaspoon black pepper
- 567 grams chicken livers, salted to taste
- oil for misting or cooking spray

### Directions:

1. Beat together eggs and water in a shallow dish. Place the flour in a separate shallow dish.
2. In the bowl of a food processor, combine the panko, plain breadcrumbs, salt, and pepper. Process until well mixed and panko crumbs are finely crushed. Place crumbs in a third shallow dish.
3. Dip livers in flour, then egg wash, and then roll in panko mixture to coat well with crumbs.
4. Spray both sides of livers with oil or cooking spray. Cooking in two batches, place livers in air fryer basket in single layer.
5. Cook at 200°C/390°F for 7 minutes. Spray livers, turn over, and spray again. Cook for 5 more minutes, until done inside and coating is golden brown.
6. Repeat to cook remaining livers.

### Variations & Ingredients Tips:

- Soak the chicken livers in milk or buttermilk for 30 minutes before coating for a milder flavor.
- Add garlic powder, onion powder, or dried herbs to the breading mixture for extra seasoning.
- Serve with hot sauce, ranch dressing, or honey mustard for dipping.

**Per Serving:** Calories: 430; Total Fat: 17g; Saturated Fat: 4.5g; Sodium: 980mg; Total Carbohydrates: 35g; Dietary Fiber: 2g; Total Sugars: 2g; Protein: 35g

## Crispy "fried" Chicken

**Servings: 4 | Prep Time: 15 Minutes | Cooking Time: 14 Minutes**

### Ingredients:

- ¾ cup all-purpose flour
- ½ teaspoon paprika
- ¼ teaspoon black pepper
- ¼ teaspoon salt
- 2 large eggs
- 1½ cups panko breadcrumbs
- 454 grams boneless, skinless chicken tenders

### Directions:

1. Preheat the air fryer to 200°C/400°F.
2. In a shallow bowl, mix the flour with the paprika, pepper, and salt.
3. In a separate bowl, whisk the eggs; set aside.
4. In a third bowl, place the breadcrumbs.
5. Liberally spray the air fryer basket with olive oil spray.
6. Pat the chicken tenders dry with a paper towel. Dredge the tenders one at a time in the flour, then dip them in the egg, and toss them in the breadcrumb coating. Repeat until all tenders are coated.
7. Set each tender in the air fryer, leaving room on each side

of the tender to allow for flipping.
8. When the basket is full, cook 4 to 7 minutes, flip, and cook another 4 to 7 minutes.
9. Remove the tenders and let cool 5 minutes before serving. Repeat until all tenders are cooked.

## Variations & Ingredients Tips:

- Add garlic powder, onion powder, or dried herbs to the flour mixture for extra flavor.
- Use crushed cornflakes or potato chips instead of breadcrumbs for a different crust.
- Serve with honey mustard, ranch dressing, or BBQ sauce for dipping.

**Per Serving:** Calories: 420; Total Fat: 11g; Saturated Fat: 2.5g; Sodium: 510mg; Total Carbohydrates: 41g; Dietary Fiber: 2g; Total Sugars: 3g; Protein: 38g

## Crispy Chicken Parmesan

**Servings: 4 | Prep Time: 15 Minutes | Cooking Time: 12 Minutes**

### Ingredients:

- 4 skinless, boneless chicken breasts, pounded thin to 0.6-cm thickness
- 1 teaspoon salt, divided
- ½ teaspoon black pepper, divided
- 1 cup flour
- 2 eggs
- 1 cup panko breadcrumbs
- ½ teaspoon dried oregano
- ½ cup grated Parmesan cheese

### Directions:

1. Pat the chicken breasts with a paper towel. Season the chicken with ½ teaspoon of the salt and ¼ teaspoon of the pepper.
2. In a medium bowl, place the flour.
3. In a second bowl, whisk the eggs.
4. In a third bowl, place the breadcrumbs, oregano, cheese, and the remaining ½ teaspoon of salt and ¼ teaspoon of pepper.
5. Dredge the chicken in the flour and shake off the excess. Dip the chicken into the eggs and then into the breadcrumbs. Set the chicken on a plate and repeat with the remaining chicken pieces.
6. Preheat the air fryer to 180°C/360°F.
7. Place the chicken in the air fryer basket and spray liberally with cooking spray. Cook for 8 minutes, turn the chicken breasts over, and cook another 4 minutes. When golden brown, check for an internal temperature of 75°C/165°F.

### Variations & Ingredients Tips:

- Use chicken thighs or cutlets instead of breasts for juicier meat.
- Add garlic powder, onion powder, or Italian seasoning to the breadcrumb mixture for extra flavor.
- Serve with marinara sauce, pesto, or a side of spaghetti for a complete meal.

**Per Serving:** Calories: 410; Total Fat: 11g; Saturated Fat: 4g; Sodium: 880mg; Total Carbohydrates: 35g; Dietary Fiber: 2g; Total Sugars: 2g; Protein: 44g

## Maple Bacon Wrapped Chicken Breasts

**Servings: 2 | Prep Time: 15 Minutes | Cooking Time: 18 Minutes**

### Ingredients:

- 2 (170g) boneless, skinless chicken breasts
- 2 tablespoons maple syrup, divided
- Freshly ground black pepper
- 6 slices thick-sliced bacon
- Fresh celery or parsley leaves
- Ranch Dressing:
- 1/4 cup mayonnaise
- 1/4 cup buttermilk
- 1/4 cup Greek yogurt
- 1 tablespoon chopped fresh chives
- 1 tablespoon chopped fresh parsley
- 1 tablespoon chopped fresh dill
- 1 tablespoon lemon juice
- Salt and freshly ground black pepper

### Directions:

1. Brush the chicken breasts with half the maple syrup and season with freshly ground black pepper. Wrap three slices of bacon around each chicken breast, securing the ends with toothpicks.
2. Preheat the air fryer to 190°C/380°F.
3. Air-fry the chicken for 6 minutes. Then turn the chicken breasts over, pour more maple syrup on top and air-fry for another 6 minutes. Turn the chicken breasts one more time, brush the remaining maple syrup all over and continue to air-fry for a final 6 minutes.
4. While the chicken is cooking, prepare the dressing by combining all the dressing ingredients together in a bowl.
5. When the chicken has finished cooking, remove the toothpicks and serve each breast with a little dressing drizzled over each one. Scatter lots of fresh celery or parsley leaves on top.

### Variations & Ingredients Tips:

- Use prosciutto or pancetta instead of bacon.
- Stuff the chicken breasts with cheese or spinach before wrapping.
- Serve with roasted sweet potatoes and green beans.

**Per Serving:** Calories: 620; Total Fat: 41g; Saturated Fat: 12g; Cholesterol: 185mg; Sodium: 1200mg; Total Carbs: 14g; Dietary Fiber: 0g; Total Sugars: 11g; Protein: 51g

## Jerk Chicken Drumsticks

**Servings: 2 | Prep Time: 10 Minutes (plus Marinating Time) | Cooking Time: 20 Minutes**

### Ingredients:

- 1 or 2 cloves garlic
- 2.5-cm of fresh ginger
- 2 serrano peppers, (with seeds if you like it spicy, seeds removed for less heat)
- 1 teaspoon ground allspice
- 1 teaspoon ground nutmeg
- 1 teaspoon chili powder
- 1/2 teaspoon dried thyme
- 1/2 teaspoon ground cinnamon
- 1/2 teaspoon paprika
- 1 tablespoon brown sugar
- 1 teaspoon soy sauce
- 2 tablespoons vegetable oil
- 6 skinless chicken drumsticks

### Directions:

1. Combine all the ingredients except the chicken in a small chopper or blender and blend to a paste. Make slashes into the meat of the chicken drumsticks and rub the spice blend all over the chicken (a pair of plastic gloves makes this really easy). Transfer the rubbed chicken to a non-reactive covered container and let the chicken marinate for at least 30 minutes or overnight in the refrigerator.
2. Preheat the air fryer to 200°C/400°F.
3. Transfer the drumsticks to the air fryer basket. Air-fry for 10 minutes. Turn the drumsticks over and air-fry for another 10 minutes.
4. Serve warm with some rice and vegetables or a green salad.

### Variations & Ingredients Tips:

- Use bone-in chicken thighs or wings instead of drumsticks.
- Add a squeeze of lime juice to the marinade for acidity.
- Serve with mango salsa or pineapple chutney.

**Per Serving:** Calories: 440; Total Fat: 28g; Saturated Fat: 6g; Cholesterol: 215mg; Sodium: 570mg; Total Carbs: 9g; Dietary Fiber: 1g; Total Sugars: 6g; Protein: 41g

# Vegetable Side Dishes Recipes

## Zucchini Fries

**Servings: 3 | Prep Time: 20 Minutes | Cooking Time: 12 Minutes**

### Ingredients:

- 1 large zucchini
- ½ cup all-purpose flour or tapioca flour
- 2 large eggs, well beaten
- 1 cup seasoned Italian-style dried bread crumbs (gluten-free, if a concern)
- Olive oil spray

### Directions:

1. Preheat the air fryer to 200°C/400°F. Trim the zucchini into a long rectangular block, taking off the ends and four "sides" to make this shape. Cut the block lengthwise into 3-cm-thick slices. Lay these slices flat and cut in half widthwise. Slice each of these pieces into 1.3-cm-thick batons. Set up and fill three shallow soup plates or small pie plates on your counter: one for the flour, one for the beaten eggs, and one for the bread crumbs. Set a zucchini baton in the flour and turn it several times to coat all sides. Gently shake off any excess flour, then dip it in the eggs, turning it to coat. Let any excess egg slip back into the rest, then set the baton in the bread crumbs and turn it several times, pressing gently to coat all sides, even the ends. Set aside on a cutting board and continue coating the remainder of the batons in the same way. Lightly coat the batons on all sides with olive oil spray. Set them in two flat layers in the basket, the top layer at a 90-degree angle to the bottom one, with a little air space between the batons in each layer. In the end, the whole thing will look like a crosshatch pattern. Air-fry undisturbed for 6 minutes. Use kitchen tongs to gently rearrange the batons so that any covered parts are now uncovered. The batons no longer need to be in a crosshatch pattern. Continue air-frying undisturbed for 6 minutes, or until lightly browned and crisp. Gently pour the contents of the basket onto a wire rack. Spread the batons out and cool for only a minute or two before serving.

### Variations & Ingredients Tips:

- Use panko breadcrumbs or crushed potato chips for a crunchier coating.
- Add grated Parmesan cheese, garlic powder, or smoked paprika to the breadcrumb mixture for extra flavor.
- Serve with marinara sauce, ranch dressing, or garlic aioli for dipping.

**Per Serving:** Calories: 255; Total Fat: 6g; Saturated Fat: 1g; Cholesterol: 124mg; Sodium: 476mg; Total Carbohydrates: 38g; Dietary Fiber: 3g; Total Sugars: 4g; Protein: 11g

## Hawaiian Brown Rice

**Servings: 4 | Prep Time: 10 Minutes | Cooking Time: 12 Minutes**

### Ingredients:

- 113g ground sausage
- 1 teaspoon butter
- 1/4 cup minced onion
- 1/4 cup minced bell pepper
- 2 cups cooked brown rice
- 227g can crushed pineapple, drained

### Directions:

1. Shape sausage into 3 or 4 thin patties. Cook at 200°C/390°F for 6 to 8 minutes or until well done. Remove from air fryer, drain, and crumble. Set aside.
2. Place butter, onion, and bell pepper in baking pan. Cook at 200°C/390°F for 1 minute and stir. Cook 4 minutes longer or just until vegetables are tender.
3. Add sausage, rice, and pineapple to vegetables and stir together.
4. Cook at 200°C/390°F for 2 minutes, until heated through.

### Variations & Ingredients Tips:

- Use chicken or pork instead of sausage.
- Add diced ham or spam for a Hawaiian twist.
- Stir in raisins, cashews or green onions.

**Per Serving:** Calories: 280; Total Fat: 10g; Saturated Fat: 3g; Cholesterol: 30mg; Sodium: 360mg; Total Carbs: 38g; Dietary Fiber: 3g; Total Sugars: 8g; Protein: 10g

## Asparagus Fries

**Servings: 4 | Prep Time: 10 Minutes | Cooking Time: 5 Minutes Per Batch**

### Ingredients:

- 340g fresh asparagus spears with tough ends trimmed off
- 2 egg whites
- ¼ cup water
- ¾ cup panko breadcrumbs
- ¼ cup grated Parmesan cheese, plus 2 tablespoons
- ¼ teaspoon salt
- Oil for misting or cooking spray

### Directions:

1. Preheat air fryer to 199°C/390°F.
2. In a shallow dish, beat egg whites and water until slightly foamy.
3. In another shallow dish, combine panko, Parmesan, and salt.
4. Dip asparagus spears in egg, then roll in crumbs. Spray with oil or cooking spray.
5. Place a layer of asparagus in air fryer basket, leaving just a little space in between each spear. Stack another layer on top, crosswise. Cook at 199°C/390°F for 5 minutes, until crispy and golden brown.
6. Repeat to cook remaining asparagus.

### Variations & Ingredients Tips:

- Use gluten-free breadcrumbs instead of panko.
- Add grated parmesan or ranch seasoning to the coating.
- Serve with a dip like ranch, marinara or cheese sauce.

**Per Serving:** Calories: 120; Total Fat: 3g; Saturated Fat: 1g; Cholesterol: 6mg; Sodium: 310mg; Total Carbs: 16g; Fiber: 2g; Sugars: 2g; Protein: 7g

## Italian Breaded Eggplant Rounds

**Servings: 4 | Prep Time: 10 Minutes | Cooking Time: 30 Minutes**

### Ingredients:

- 1 eggplant, sliced into rounds
- 1 egg
- 1/2 cup bread crumbs
- 1 tsp onion powder
- 1/2 tsp Italian seasoning
- 1/2 tsp garlic salt
- 1/2 tsp paprika
- 1 tbsp olive oil

### Directions:

1. Preheat air fryer to 180°C/360°F.
2. Whisk the egg and 1 tbsp of water in a bowl until frothy.
3. Mix the bread crumbs, onion powder, Italian seasoning, salt, and paprika in a separate bowl.
4. Dip the eggplant slices into the egg mixture, then coat them into the bread crumb mixture.
5. Put the slices in a single layer in the frying basket. Drizzle with olive oil.
6. Air fry for 23-25 minutes, turning once.
7. Serve warm.

### Variations & Ingredients Tips:

- Use panko breadcrumbs for extra crispiness.
- Add grated parmesan to the breadcrumb mixture.
- Serve with marinara sauce for dipping.

**Per Serving:** Calories: 155; Total Fat: 5g; Saturated Fat: 1g; Cholesterol: 54mg; Sodium: 498mg; Total Carbs: 23g; Dietary Fiber: 4g; Total Sugars: 5g; Protein: 5g

## Lemony Green Bean Sauté

**Servings: 6 | Prep Time: 10 Minutes | Cooking Time: 15 Minutes**

### Ingredients:

- 1 tbsp chopped cilantro
- 454g green beans, trimmed
- 1/2 red onion, sliced
- 2 tbsp olive oil
- Salt and pepper to taste
- 1 tbsp grapefruit juice
- 6 lemon wedges

### Directions:

1. Preheat air fryer to 180°C/360°F.
2. Coat the green beans, red onion, olive oil, salt, pepper, cilantro and grapefruit juice in a bowl.
3. Pour the mixture into the air fryer and bake for 5 minutes.
4. Stir well and cook for 5 minutes more.
5. Serve with lemon wedges.

### Variations & Ingredients Tips:

- Use orange or lime juice instead of grapefruit.
- Add sliced almonds or crumbled feta for crunch and flavor.
- Toss with balsamic vinegar before serving.

**Per Serving:** Calories: 65; Total Fat: 4g; Saturated Fat: 0.5g; Cholesterol: 0mg; Sodium: 30mg; Total Carbs: 7g; Dietary Fiber: 3g; Total Sugars: 3g; Protein: 2g

## Grits Casserole

**Servings: 4 | Prep Time: 10 Minutes | Cooking Time: 30 Minutes**

### Ingredients:

- 10 fresh asparagus spears, cut into 2.5-cm pieces
- 2 cups cooked grits, cooled to room temperature
- 1 egg, beaten
- 2 teaspoons Worcestershire sauce
- 1/2 teaspoon garlic powder
- 1/4 teaspoon salt
- 2 slices provolone cheese (about 1 15-g)
- Oil for misting or cooking spray

### Directions:

1. Mist asparagus spears with oil and cook at 200°C/390°F for 5 minutes, until crisp-tender.
2. In a medium bowl, mix together the grits, egg, Worcestershire, garlic powder, and salt.
3. Spoon half of grits mixture into air fryer baking pan and top with asparagus.
4. Tear cheese slices into pieces and layer evenly on top of asparagus.
5. Top with remaining grits.
6. Bake at 180°C/360°F for 25 minutes. The casserole will rise a little as it cooks. When done, the top will have browned lightly with just a hint of crispiness.

### Variations & Ingredients Tips:

- Substitute broccoli, spinach or mushrooms for the asparagus.
- Use different cheese varieties like cheddar or pepper jack.

- Add crumbled bacon or ham to the grits mixture.

**Per Serving:** Calories: 210; Total Fat: 8g; Saturated Fat: 4g; Cholesterol: 65mg; Sodium: 420mg; Total Carbohydrates: 26g; Dietary Fiber: 1g; Total Sugars: 1g; Protein: 9g

## Toasted Choco-nuts

**Servings: 2 | Prep Time: 5 Minutes | Cooking Time: 10 Minutes**

### Ingredients:

- 2 cups almonds
- 2 teaspoons maple syrup
- 2 tablespoons cacao powder

### Directions:

1. Preheat air fryer to 180°C/350°F.
2. Distribute the almonds in a single layer in the frying basket and Bake for 3 minutes.
3. Shake the basket and Bake for another 1 minute until golden brown.
4. Remove them to a bowl. Drizzle with maple syrup and toss.
5. Sprinkle with cacao powder and toss until well coated.
6. Let cool completely.
7. Store in a container at room temperature for up to 2 weeks or in the fridge for up to a month.

### Variations & Ingredients Tips:

- Use different types of nuts, such as cashews or pecans, for a variety of flavors and textures.
- Add some ground cinnamon or vanilla extract for extra flavor.
- For a savory version, replace the maple syrup and cacao powder with olive oil and your favorite spice blend.

**Per Serving:** Calories: 580; Total Fat: 51g; Saturated Fat: 4g; Cholesterol: 0mg; Sodium: 0mg; Total Carbs: 27g; Fiber: 13g; Sugars: 9g; Protein: 21g

## Dijon Roasted Purple Potatoes

**Servings: 4 | Prep Time: 10 Minutes | Cooking Time: 25 Minutes**

### Ingredients:

- 454g purple potatoes, scrubbed and halved
- 1 tbsp olive oil
- 1 tsp Dijon mustard
- 1 tsp lemon juice
- 2 cloves garlic, minced
- Salt and pepper to taste
- 2 tbsp butter, melted
- 1 tbsp chopped cilantro
- 1 tsp fresh rosemary

### Directions:

1. Mix the olive oil, mustard, garlic, lemon juice, pepper, salt

and rosemary in a bowl. Chill covered until ready to use.
2. Preheat air fryer at 177°C/350°F.
3. Toss the potatoes, salt, pepper, and butter in a bowl.
4. Place potatoes in the frying basket, and Roast for 18-20 minutes, tossing once.
5. Transfer potatoes to a bowl. Drizzle with the dressing and toss to coat.
6. Garnish with cilantro to serve.

### Variations & Ingredients Tips:

- Use Yukon gold or fingerling potatoes instead of purple.
- Add whole grain mustard or horseradish to the dressing.
- Sprinkle with crispy shallots or bacon bits.

**Per Serving:** Calories: 210; Total Fat: 12g; Saturated Fat: 5g; Cholesterol: 15mg; Sodium: 160mg; Total Carbs: 24g; Fiber: 3g; Sugars: 2g; Protein: 3g

## Roasted Garlic And Thyme Tomatoes

**Servings: 2 | Prep Time: 5 Minutes | Cooking Time: 15 Minutes**

### Ingredients:

- 4 Roma tomatoes
- 1 tablespoon olive oil
- Salt and freshly ground black pepper
- 1 clove garlic, minced
- 1/2 teaspoon dried thyme

### Directions:

1. Preheat air fryer to 199°C/390°F.
2. Cut tomatoes in half and scoop out seeds/pithy parts.
3. In a bowl, toss tomatoes with olive oil, salt, pepper, garlic and thyme.
4. Transfer tomatoes cut-side up to air fryer basket.
5. Air fry for 15 minutes until edges just start to brown.
6. Let cool slightly before serving.

### Variations & Ingredients Tips:

- Use cherry or grape tomatoes instead of Roma.
- Add balsamic vinegar or red pepper flakes for extra flavor.
- Top with grated parmesan or mozzarella before serving.

**Per Serving:** Calories: 71; Total Fat: 5g; Saturated Fat: 1g; Cholesterol: 0mg; Sodium: 7mg; Total Carbohydrates: 6g; Dietary Fiber: 2g; Total Sugars: 4g; Protein: 1g

## Tuna Platter

**Servings: 4 | Prep Time: 20 Minutes | Cooking Time: 9 Minutes**

### Ingredients:

- 4 new potatoes, boiled in their jackets
- ½ cup vinaigrette dressing, plus 2 tablespoons
- 225 g fresh green beans, cut in 1.3-cm pieces and steamed
- 1 tbsp Herbes de Provence
- 1 tbsp minced shallots
- 1½ tbsp tarragon vinegar
- 4 tuna steaks, each 2-cm thick, about 450 g
- salt and pepper
- Salad
- 8 cups chopped romaine lettuce
- 12 grape tomatoes, halved lengthwise
- ½ cup pitted olives (black, green, nicoise, or combination)
- 2 boiled eggs, peeled and halved lengthwise

### Directions:

1. Quarter potatoes and toss with 1 tablespoon salad dressing. Toss the warm beans with the other tablespoon of salad dressing. Set both aside while you prepare the tuna. Mix together the herbs, shallots, and vinegar and rub into all sides of tuna. Season fish to taste with salt and pepper. Cook tuna at 200°C/390°F for 7 minutes and check. If needed, cook 2 minutes longer, until tuna is barely pink in the center. Spread the lettuce over a large platter. Slice the tuna steaks in 3-cm pieces and arrange them in the center of the lettuce. Place the remaining ingredients around the tuna. Diners create their own plates by selecting what they want from the platter. Pass remainder of salad dressing at the table.

### Variations & Ingredients Tips:

- Use salmon, swordfish, or mahi-mahi instead of tuna for a different fish option.
- Add marinated artichoke hearts, roasted red peppers, or capers to the platter for extra Mediterranean flavors.
- Serve with a lemon wedge and crusty bread on the side.

**Per Serving:** Calories: 470; Total Fat: 23g; Saturated Fat: 4g; Cholesterol: 157mg; Sodium: 621mg; Total Carbohydrates: 25g; Dietary Fiber: 6g; Total Sugars: 5g; Protein: 42g

## Cholula Onion Rings

**Servings: 4 | Prep Time: 10 Minutes | Cooking Time: 30 Minutes**

### Ingredients:

- 1 large Vidalia onion
- ½ cup chickpea flour
- 1/3 cup milk
- 2 tbsp lemon juice
- 2 tbsp Cholula hot sauce
- 1 tsp allspice
- 2/3 cup bread crumbs

### Directions:

1. Preheat air fryer to 193°C/380°F.
2. Cut 1 cm off the top of the onion's root, then cut into 1.3cm thick rings. Set aside.
3. Combine the chickpea flour, milk, lemon juice, hot sauce, and allspice in a bowl.
4. In another bowl, add in breadcrumbs.

5. Submerge each ring into the flour batter until well coated, then dip into the breadcrumbs.
6. Air Fry for 14 minutes until crispy, turning once.
7. Serve.

### Variations & Ingredients Tips:

- Use panko breadcrumbs for extra crunch.
- Substitute buttermilk for the regular milk.
- Add cajun seasoning or ranch dressing mix to the breadcrumbs.

**Per Serving:** Calories: 195; Total Fat: 4g; Saturated Fat: 1g; Cholesterol: 2mg; Sodium: 255mg; Total Carbs: 35g; Fiber: 4g; Sugars: 6g; Protein: 6g

## Spicy Fried Green Beans

**Servings: 2 | Prep Time: 5 Minutes | Cooking Time: 8 Minutes**

### Ingredients:

- 340 g green beans, trimmed
- 2 small dried hot red chili peppers (like árbol)
- 60 ml panko breadcrumbs
- 1 tablespoon olive oil
- ½ teaspoon salt
- ⅛ teaspoon crushed red pepper flakes
- 2 scallions, thinly sliced

### Directions:

1. Preheat the air fryer to 200°C/400°F.
2. Toss the green beans, chili peppers and panko breadcrumbs with the olive oil, salt and crushed red pepper flakes.
3. Air-fry for 8 minutes (depending on the size of the beans), shaking the basket once during the cooking process. The crumbs will fall into the bottom drawer – don't worry.
4. Transfer the green beans to a serving dish, sprinkle the scallions and the toasted crumbs from the air fryer drawer on top and serve. The dried peppers are not to be eaten, but they do look nice with the green beans. You can leave them in, or take them out as you please.

### Variations & Ingredients Tips:

- Use different types of breadcrumbs, such as regular or Italian-seasoned, for a variety of flavors and textures.
- Add some grated Parmesan cheese or nutritional yeast for a cheesy flavor.
- Serve the green beans with a dipping sauce, such as ranch dressing or garlic aioli.

**Per Serving:** Calories: 130; Total Fat: 7g; Saturated Fat: 1g; Cholesterol: 0mg; Sodium: 620mg; Total Carbs: 14g; Fiber: 4g; Sugars: 4g; Protein: 4g

## Garlicky Brussels Sprouts

**Servings: 4 | Prep Time: 10 Minutes | Cooking Time: 35 Minutes**

### Ingredients:

- 454g Brussels sprouts, halved lengthwise
- 1 tbsp olive oil
- 1 tbsp lemon juice
- ½ tsp sea salt
- ⅛ tsp garlic powder
- 4 garlic cloves, sliced
- 2 tbsp parsley, chopped
- ½ tsp red chili flakes

### Directions:

1. Preheat air fryer to 190°C/375°F.
2. Combine the olive oil, lemon juice, salt, and garlic powder in a bowl. Add sprouts and toss to coat.
3. Put sprouts in the frying basket. Air Fry 15-20 mins, shaking once until golden and crisp.
4. Sprinkle with garlic slices, parsley, and chili flakes. Toss and cook 2-4 mins more until garlic browns slightly.

### Variations & Ingredients Tips:

- Add grated parmesan or panko breadcrumbs for crunch.
- Substitute balsamic vinegar for some of the oil.
- Use pre-shredded brussels sprout pieces for faster cooking.

**Per Serving:** Calories: 90; Total Fat: 5g; Saturated Fat: 1g; Cholesterol: 0mg; Sodium: 290mg; Total Carbs: 10g; Fiber: 4g; Sugars: 2g; Protein: 4g

## Broccoli Au Gratin

**Servings: 2 | Prep Time: 10 Minutes | Cooking Time: 25 Minutes**

### Ingredients:

- 2 cups broccoli florets, chopped
- 6 tbsp grated Gruyère cheese
- 1 tbsp grated Pecorino cheese
- ½ tbsp olive oil
- 1 tbsp flour
- 1/3 cup milk
- ½ tsp ground coriander
- Salt and black pepper
- 2 tbsp panko bread crumbs

### Directions:

1. Whisk the olive oil, flour, milk, coriander, salt, and pepper in a bowl.
2. Incorporate broccoli, Gruyere cheese, panko bread crumbs, and Pecorino cheese until well combined.
3. Pour in a greased baking dish.
4. Preheat air fryer to 165°C/330°F.
5. Put the baking dish into the frying basket. Bake until the broccoli is crisp-tender and the top is golden, or about 12-15 minutes.

6. Serve warm.

### Variations & Ingredients Tips:

- Use a mix of cheddar and parmesan cheeses.
- Add sautéed mushrooms or caramelized onions to the mixture.
- Top with crushed crackers or fried onion strings before baking.

**Per Serving:** Calories: 240; Total Fat: 14g; Saturated Fat: 6g; Cholesterol: 30mg; Sodium: 320mg; Total Carbs: 18g; Fiber: 4g; Sugars: 4g; Protein: 13g

## Mediterranean Roasted Vegetables

**Servings: 4 | Prep Time: 10 Minutes | Cooking Time: 30 Minutes**

### Ingredients:

- 1 red bell pepper, cut into chunks
- 1 cup sliced mushrooms
- 1 cup green beans, diced
- 1 zucchini, sliced
- 1/3 cup diced red onion
- 3 garlic cloves, sliced
- 2 tbsp olive oil
- 1 tsp rosemary
- 1/2 tsp flaked sea salt

### Directions:

1. Preheat air fryer to 180°C/350°F.
2. Add the bell pepper, mushrooms, green beans, red onion, zucchini, rosemary, and garlic to a bowl and mix.
3. Spritz with olive oil and stir until well-coated.
4. Put the veggies in the frying basket and air fry for 14-18 minutes until crispy and softened.
5. Serve sprinkled with flaked sea salt.

### Variations & Ingredients Tips:

- Add diced eggplant or cherry tomatoes.
- Use balsamic vinegar instead of olive oil.
- Toss with fresh basil or parmesan after cooking.

**Per Serving:** Calories: 88; Total Fat: 5g; Saturated Fat: 1g; Cholesterol: 0mg; Sodium: 106mg; Total Carbohydrates: 10g; Dietary Fiber: 3g; Total Sugars: 5g; Protein: 3g

## Fried Eggplant Balls

**Servings: 4 | Prep Time: 20 Minutes | Cooking Time: 40 Minutes**

### Ingredients:

- 1 medium eggplant (about 454g)
- Olive oil
- Salt and freshly ground black pepper
- 1 cup grated Parmesan cheese
- 2 cups fresh breadcrumbs
- 2 tablespoons chopped fresh parsley
- 2 tablespoons chopped fresh basil
- 1 clove garlic, minced
- 1 egg, lightly beaten
- ½ cup fine dried breadcrumbs

### Directions:

1. Preheat the air fryer to 200°C/400°F.
2. Quarter the eggplant. Make slashes in the flesh but not through the skin. Brush cut sides with olive oil. Transfer to air fryer basket, cut side up. Air-fry 10 minutes.
3. Flip eggplant, air-fry 15 more minutes until soft. Cool on cutting board.
4. In a food processor, combine Parmesan, fresh breadcrumbs, herbs, garlic and egg. Scoop out 1-1½ cups eggplant flesh and add to processor. Season with salt and pepper. Process until smooth. Refrigerate 30 minutes.
5. Place dried breadcrumbs in a dish. Scoop eggplant mixture and roll in breadcrumbs to form 16-18 balls. Refrigerate until ready to fry.
6. Preheat air fryer to 177°C/350°F. Spray eggplant balls and basket with oil. Air fry 15 minutes, rotating frequently to brown evenly.

### Variations & Ingredients Tips:

- Add sun-dried tomatoes or olives to the eggplant mixture.
- Use panko breadcrumbs for extra crunch.
- Serve with marinara sauce for dipping.

**Per Serving:** Calories: 360; Total Fat: 14g; Saturated Fat: 4g; Cholesterol: 60mg; Sodium: 870mg; Total Carbs: 48g; Fiber: 8g; Sugars: 9g; Protein: 14g

## Roman Artichokes

**Servings: 4 | Prep Time: 5 Minutes | Cooking Time: 12 Minutes**

### Ingredients:

- 2 (255g) boxes frozen artichoke heart quarters, thawed
- 1 1/2 tablespoons olive oil
- 2 teaspoons minced garlic
- 1 teaspoon table salt
- Up to 1/2 teaspoon red pepper flakes

### Directions:

1. Preheat air fryer to 200°C/400°F.
2. In a bowl, gently toss artichoke hearts with oil, garlic, salt and red pepper flakes until coated.
3. When preheated, spread artichokes in air fryer basket in a single layer.
4. Air fry undisturbed for 8 minutes.
5. Gently toss and rearrange artichokes. Cook 4 more minutes until very crisp.
6. Transfer to a wire rack and cool briefly before serving.

### Variations & Ingredients Tips:

- Use fresh quartered artichoke hearts if available.
- Add lemon zest or juice to the tossing mixture.
- Sprinkle with grated parmesan after cooking.

**Per Serving:** Calories: 107; Total Fat: 7g; Saturated Fat: 1g; Cholesterol: 0mg; Sodium: 438mg; Total Carbohydrates: 10g; Dietary Fiber: 6g; Total Sugars: 2g; Protein: 3g

## Buttery Stuffed Tomatoes

**Servings: 6 | Prep Time: 10 Minutes | Cooking Time: 15 Minutes**

### Ingredients:

- 3 227g round tomatoes
- ½ cup plus 1 tablespoon Plain panko bread crumbs (gluten-free, if a concern)
- 3 tablespoons (about 14g) Finely grated Parmesan cheese
- 3 tablespoons Butter, melted and cooled
- 4 teaspoons Stemmed and chopped fresh parsley leaves
- 1 teaspoon Minced garlic
- ¼ teaspoon Table salt
- Up to ¼ teaspoon Red pepper flakes
- Olive oil spray

### Directions:

1. Preheat the air fryer to 190°C/375°F.
2. Cut the tomatoes in half through their "equators" (that is, not through the stem ends). One at a time, gently squeeze the tomato halves over a trash can, using a clean finger to gently force out the seeds and most of the juice inside, working carefully so that the tomato doesn't lose its round shape or get crushed.
3. Stir the bread crumbs, cheese, butter, parsley, garlic, salt, and red pepper flakes in a bowl until the bread crumbs are moistened and the parsley is uniform throughout the mixture. Pile this mixture into the spaces left in the tomato halves. Press gently to compact the filling. Coat the tops of the tomatoes with olive oil spray.
4. Place the tomatoes cut side up in the basket. They may touch each other. Air-fry for 15 minutes, or until the filling is lightly browned and crunchy.
5. Use nonstick-safe spatula and kitchen tongs for balance to gently transfer the stuffed tomatoes to a platter or a cutting board. Cool for a couple of minutes before serving.

### Variations & Ingredients Tips:

- Add crumbled feta or gorgonzola to the bread crumb mixture.
- Substitute basil or oregano for the parsley.
- Drizzle with balsamic glaze before serving.

**Per Serving:** Calories: 135; Total Fat: 7g; Saturated Fat: 3g; Cholesterol: 13mg; Sodium: 310mg; Total Carbs: 15g; Fiber: 2g; Sugars: 4g; Protein: 4g

## Honey-roasted Parsnips

**Servings: 3 | Prep Time: 10 Minutes | Cooking Time: 23 Minutes**

### Ingredients:

- 680g medium parsnips, peeled
- Olive oil spray
- 1 tablespoon honey
- 1 1/2 teaspoons water
- 1/4 teaspoon table salt

### Directions:

1. Preheat the air fryer to 177°C/350°F.
2. If the thick end of a parsnip is more than 1.25cm in diameter, cut just below where it swells to the large end, then slice the large section in half lengthwise.
3. If parsnips are larger than the basket, trim off the thin end so they fit. Generously coat all sides with olive oil spray.
4. When machine is at temperature, set parsnips in basket with space between them. Air fry undisturbed for 20 minutes.
5. Whisk the honey, water, and salt in a small bowl until smooth. Brush this mixture over the parsnips.
6. Air fry undisturbed for 3 minutes more, or until the glaze is lightly browned.
7. Use tongs to transfer parsnips to a wire rack or serving platter. Cool for a couple of minutes before serving.

### Variations & Ingredients Tips:

- Add cinnamon or nutmeg to the glaze for warmth.
- Substitute maple syrup for the honey.
- Toss with chopped parsley or thyme after roasting.

**Per Serving:** Calories: 131; Total Fat: 0.2g; Saturated Fat: 0g; Cholesterol: 0mg; Sodium: 156mg; Total Carbs: 31g; Dietary Fiber: 7g; Total Sugars: 14g; Protein: 2g

## Roasted Peppers With Balsamic Vinegar And Basil

**Servings: 6 | Prep Time: 10 Minutes | Cooking Time: 12 Minutes**

### Ingredients:

- 4 small or medium red or yellow bell peppers
- 3 tablespoons olive oil
- 1 tablespoon balsamic vinegar
- Up to 6 fresh basil leaves, torn

### Directions:

1. Preheat air fryer to 200°C/400°F.
2. When preheated, place whole peppers in air fryer basket with 6mm space between them.
3. Air fry undisturbed for 12 minutes until blistered and blackened in spots.

4. Transfer peppers to a bowl and cover with plastic wrap. Let sit 30 minutes.
5. Uncover and peel off skin from peppers. Remove stem ends, seeds and membranes.
6. Slice peppers into strips and place in a clean bowl.
7. Gently toss with olive oil, balsamic vinegar and torn basil leaves.
8. Serve immediately or refrigerate for up to 5 days.

**Variations & Ingredients Tips:**

- Use a mix of colored bell peppers.
- Add minced garlic or red pepper flakes for extra flavor.
- Top with crumbled feta or shaved parmesan.

**Per Serving:** Calories: 88; Total Fat: 8g; Saturated Fat: 1g; Cholesterol: 0mg; Sodium: 3mg; Total Carbohydrates: 4g; Dietary Fiber: 1g; Total Sugars: 3g; Protein: 1g

# Sandwiches And Burgers Recipes

## Chili Cheese Dogs

**Servings: 3 | Prep Time: 10 Minutes | Cooking Time: 12 Minutes**

**Ingredients:**

- 340 grams Lean ground beef
- 1½ tablespoons Chile powder
- 240 grams plus 2 tablespoons Jarred sofrito
- 3 Hot dogs (gluten-free, if a concern)
- 3 Hot dog buns (gluten-free, if a concern), split open lengthwise
- 3 tablespoons Finely chopped scallion
- 60 grams Shredded Cheddar cheese

**Directions:**

1. Crumble the ground beef into a medium or large saucepan set over medium heat. Brown well, stirring often to break up the clumps. Add the chile powder and cook for 30 seconds, stirring the whole time. Stir in the sofrito and bring to a simmer. Reduce the heat to low and simmer, stirring occasionally, for 5 minutes. Keep warm.
2. Preheat the air fryer to 200°C/400°F.
3. When the machine is at temperature, put the hot dogs in the basket and air-fry undisturbed for 10 minutes, or until the hot dogs are bubbling and blistered, even a little crisp.
4. Use kitchen tongs to put the hot dogs in the buns. Top each with about 120 grams of the ground beef mixture, 1 tablespoon of the minced scallion, and 20 grams of the cheese. (The scallion should go under the cheese so it superheats and wilts a bit.) Set the filled hot dog buns in the basket and air-fry undisturbed for 2 minutes, or until the cheese has melted.
5. Remove the basket from the machine. Cool the chili cheese dogs in the basket for 5 minutes before serving.

**Variations & Ingredients Tips:**

- Use turkey or veggie hot dogs for a healthier option.
- Substitute cheddar cheese with your favorite melty cheese, such as pepper jack or Swiss.
- Add diced onions or jalapeños to the chili for extra flavor and heat.

**Per Serving:** Calories: 580; Cholesterol: 110mg; Total Fat: 32g; Saturated Fat: 13g; Sodium: 1420mg; Total Carbohydrates: 36g; Dietary Fiber: 5g; Total Sugars: 6g; Protein: 38g

## Chicken Apple Brie Melt

**Servings: 3 | Prep Time: 10 Minutes | Cooking Time: 13 Minutes**

**Ingredients:**

- 3 140 to 170-gram boneless skinless chicken breasts
- Vegetable oil spray
- 1½ teaspoons Dried herbes de Provence
- 85 grams Brie, rind removed, thinly sliced
- 6 Thin cored apple slices
- 3 French rolls (gluten-free, if a concern)
- 2 tablespoons Dijon mustard (gluten-free, if a concern)

**Directions:**

1. Preheat the air fryer to 190°C/375°F.
2. Lightly coat all sides of the chicken breasts with vegetable oil spray. Sprinkle the breasts evenly with the herbes de Provence.
3. When the machine is at temperature, set the breasts in the basket and air-fry undisturbed for 10 minutes.
4. Top the chicken breasts with the apple slices, then the cheese. Air-fry undisturbed for 2 minutes, or until the cheese is melty and bubbling.
5. Use a nonstick-safe spatula and kitchen tongs, for balance, to transfer the breasts to a cutting board. Set the rolls in the basket and air-fry for 1 minute to warm through. (Putting them in the machine without splitting them keeps the insides very soft while the outside gets a little crunchy.)

6. Transfer the rolls to the cutting board. Split them open lengthwise, then spread 1 teaspoon mustard on each cut side. Set a prepared chicken breast on the bottom of a roll and close with its top, repeating as necessary to make additional sandwiches. Serve warm.

### Variations & Ingredients Tips:

- Substitute the Brie with Camembert or another soft cheese of your choice.
- Use pears instead of apples for a different flavor profile.
- Add baby spinach or arugula for extra greens and nutrition.

**Per Serving:** Calories: 510; Cholesterol: 135mg; Total Fat: 19g; Saturated Fat: 8g; Sodium: 670mg; Total Carbohydrates: 41g; Dietary Fiber: 2g; Total Sugars: 6g; Protein: 45g

## Chicken Spiedies

**Servings: 3 | Prep Time: 15 Minutes (plus Marinating Time) | Cooking Time: 12 Minutes**

### Ingredients:

- 570 grams Boneless skinless chicken thighs, trimmed of any fat blobs and cut into 5-cm pieces
- 3 tablespoons Red wine vinegar
- 2 tablespoons Olive oil
- 2 tablespoons Minced fresh mint leaves
- 2 tablespoons Minced fresh parsley leaves
- 2 teaspoons Minced fresh dill fronds
- ¾ teaspoon Fennel seeds
- ¾ teaspoon Table salt
- Up to a ¼ teaspoon Red pepper flakes
- 3 Long soft rolls, such as hero, hoagie, or Italian sub rolls (gluten-free, if a concern), split open lengthwise
- 4½ tablespoons Regular or low-fat mayonnaise (not fat-free; gluten-free, if a concern)
- 1½ tablespoons Distilled white vinegar
- 1½ teaspoons Ground black pepper

### Directions:

1. Mix the chicken, vinegar, oil, mint, parsley, dill, fennel seeds, salt, and red pepper flakes in a zip-closed plastic bag. Seal, gently massage the marinade ingredients into the meat, and refrigerate for at least 2 hours or up to 6 hours. (Longer than that and the meat can turn rubbery.)
2. Set the plastic bag out on the counter (to make the contents a little less frigid). Preheat the air fryer to 200°C/400°F.
3. When the machine is at temperature, use kitchen tongs to set the chicken thighs in the basket (discard any remaining marinade) and air-fry undisturbed for 6 minutes. Turn the thighs over and continue air-frying undisturbed for 6 minutes more, until well browned, cooked through, and even a little crunchy.
4. Dump the contents of the basket onto a wire rack and cool for 2 or 3 minutes. Divide the chicken evenly between the rolls. Whisk the mayonnaise, vinegar, and black pepper in a small bowl until smooth. Drizzle this sauce over the chicken pieces in the rolls.

### Variations & Ingredients Tips:

- Use chicken breast instead of thighs for a leaner option.
- Substitute the herbs with your favorite combination, such as basil, oregano, or thyme.
- Add sliced onions or pickled vegetables for extra crunch and tanginess.

**Per Serving:** Calories: 710; Cholesterol: 200mg; Total Fat: 44g; Saturated Fat: 8g; Sodium: 1240mg; Total Carbohydrates: 37g; Dietary Fiber: 2g; Total Sugars: 4g; Protein: 45g

## Eggplant Parmesan Subs

**Servings: 2 | Prep Time: 10 Minutes | Cooking Time: 13 Minutes**

### Ingredients:

- 4 Peeled eggplant slices (about 1.25 cm thick and 7.5 cm in diameter)
- Olive oil spray
- 2 tablespoons plus 2 teaspoons Jarred pizza sauce, any variety except creamy
- ¼ cup (about 20 grams) Finely grated Parmesan cheese
- 2 Small, long soft rolls, such as hero, hoagie, or Italian sub rolls (gluten-free, if a concern), split open lengthwise

### Directions:

1. Preheat the air fryer to 175°C/350°F.
2. When the machine is at temperature, coat both sides of the eggplant slices with olive oil spray. Set them in the basket in one layer and air-fry undisturbed for 10 minutes, until lightly browned and softened.
3. Increase the machine's temperature to 190°C/375°F (or 185°C/370°F, if that's the closest setting—unless the machine is already at 180°C/360°F, in which case leave it alone). Top each eggplant slice with 2 teaspoons pizza sauce, then 1 tablespoon of cheese. Air-fry undisturbed for 2 minutes, or until the cheese has melted.
4. Use a nonstick-safe spatula, and perhaps a flatware fork for balance, to transfer the eggplant slices cheese side up to a cutting board. Set the roll(s) cut side down in the basket in one layer (working in batches as necessary) and air-fry undisturbed for 1 minute, to toast the rolls a bit and warm them up. Set 2 eggplant slices in each warm roll.

### Variations & Ingredients Tips:

- Use zucchini slices instead of eggplant for a different vegetable option.
- Add a slice of fresh mozzarella on top of the Parmesan for extra cheesiness.
- Sprinkle some dried herbs like oregano or basil on the eggplant before cooking for extra flavor.

**Per Serving (1 sandwich):** Calories: 280; Cholesterol: 10mg;

Total Fat: 9g; Saturated Fat: 3g; Sodium: 840mg; Total Carbohydrates: 40g; Dietary Fiber: 5g; Total Sugars: 8g; Protein: 11g

## Provolone Stuffed Meatballs

**Servings: 4 | Prep Time: 20 Minutes | Cooking Time: 12 Minutes**

### Ingredients:

- 1 tablespoon olive oil
- 1 small onion, very finely chopped
- 1 to 2 cloves garlic, minced
- 340 grams ground beef
- 340 grams ground pork
- ¾ cup breadcrumbs
- ¼ cup grated Parmesan cheese
- ¼ cup finely chopped fresh parsley (or 1 tablespoon dried parsley)
- ½ teaspoon dried oregano
- 1½ teaspoons salt
- freshly ground black pepper
- 2 eggs, lightly beaten
- 140 grams sharp or aged provolone cheese, cut into 2.5-cm cubes

### Directions:

1. Preheat a skillet over medium-high heat. Add the oil and cook the onion and garlic until tender, but not browned.
2. Transfer the onion and garlic to a large bowl and add the beef, pork, breadcrumbs, Parmesan cheese, parsley, oregano, salt, pepper and eggs. Mix well until all the ingredients are combined. Divide the mixture into 12 evenly sized balls. Make one meatball at a time, by pressing a hole in the meatball mixture with your finger and pushing a piece of provolone cheese into the hole. Mold the meat back into a ball, enclosing the cheese.
3. Preheat the air fryer to 190°C/380°F.
4. Working in two batches, transfer six of the meatballs to the air fryer basket and air-fry for 12 minutes, shaking the basket and turning the meatballs a couple of times during the cooking process. Repeat with the remaining six meatballs. You can pop the first batch of meatballs into the air fryer for the last two minutes of cooking to re-heat them. Serve warm.

### Variations & Ingredients Tips:

- Substitute beef and pork with ground turkey or chicken for a leaner meatball option.
- Use mozzarella or fontina cheese instead of provolone for a milder flavor.
- Serve meatballs with marinara sauce, in sub rolls, or over pasta for a complete meal.

**Per Serving (3 meatballs):** Calories: 520; Cholesterol: 180mg; Total Fat: 36g; Saturated Fat: 15g; Sodium: 1160mg; Total Carbohydrates: 18g; Dietary Fiber: 1g; Total Sugars: 2g; Protein: 35g

## Salmon Burgers

**Servings: 3 | Prep Time: 15 Minutes | Cooking Time: 8 Minutes**

### Ingredients:

- 510 grams Skinless salmon fillet, preferably fattier Atlantic salmon
- 1½ tablespoons Minced chives or the green part of a scallion
- ½ cup Plain panko bread crumbs (gluten-free, if a concern)
- 1½ teaspoons Dijon mustard (gluten-free, if a concern)
- 1½ teaspoons Drained and rinsed capers, minced
- 1½ teaspoons Lemon juice
- ¼ teaspoon Table salt
- ¼ teaspoon Ground black pepper
- Vegetable oil spray

### Directions:

1. Preheat the air fryer to 190°C/375°F.
2. Cut the salmon into pieces that will fit in a food processor. Cover and pulse until coarsely chopped. Add the chives and pulse to combine, until the fish is ground but not a paste. Scrape down and remove the blade. Scrape the salmon mixture into a bowl. Add the bread crumbs, mustard, capers, lemon juice, salt, and pepper. Stir gently until well combined.
3. Use clean and dry hands to form the mixture into two 12.5-cm patties for a small batch, three 12.5-cm patties for a medium batch, or four 12.5-cm patties for a large one.
4. Coat both sides of each patty with vegetable oil spray. Set them in the basket in one layer and air-fry undisturbed for 8 minutes, or until browned and an instant-read meat thermometer inserted into the center of a burger registers 65°C/145°F.
5. Use a nonstick-safe spatula, and perhaps a flatware fork for balance, to transfer the burgers to a wire rack. Cool for 2 or 3 minutes before serving.

### Variations & Ingredients Tips:

- Substitute salmon with canned or leftover cooked salmon for convenience.
- Add finely chopped red bell pepper or celery to the burger mixture for extra crunch and flavor.
- Serve on toasted buns with lettuce, tomato, and a dollop of tartar sauce or remoulade.

**Per Serving (1 burger):** Calories: 320; Cholesterol: 95mg; Total Fat: 16g; Saturated Fat: 3g; Sodium: 440mg; Total Carbohydrates: 15g; Dietary Fiber: 1g; Total Sugars: 1g; Protein: 31g

## Thanksgiving Turkey Sandwiches

**Servings: 3 | Prep Time: 15 Minutes | Cooking Time: 10 Minutes**

### Ingredients:

- 1½ cups Herb-seasoned stuffing mix (not cornbread-style; gluten-free, if a concern)
- 1 Large egg white(s)
- 2 tablespoons Water
- 3 140- to 170-gram turkey breast cutlets
- Vegetable oil spray
- 4½ tablespoons Purchased cranberry sauce, preferably whole berry
- ⅛ teaspoon Ground cinnamon
- ⅛ teaspoon Ground dried ginger
- 4½ tablespoons Regular, low-fat, or fat-free mayonnaise (gluten-free, if a concern)
- 6 tablespoons Shredded Brussels sprouts
- 3 Kaiser rolls (gluten-free, if a concern), split open

### Directions:

1. Preheat the air fryer to 190°C/375°F.
2. Put the stuffing mix in a heavy zip-closed bag, seal it, lay it flat on your counter, and roll a rolling pin over the bag to crush the stuffing mix to the consistency of rough sand. (Or you can pulse the stuffing mix to the desired consistency in a food processor.)
3. Set up and fill two shallow soup plates or small pie plates on your counter: one for the egg white(s), whisked with the water until foamy; and one for the ground stuffing mix.
4. Dip a cutlet in the egg white mixture, coating both sides and letting any excess egg white slip back into the rest. Set the cutlet in the ground stuffing mix and coat it evenly on both sides, pressing gently to coat well on both sides. Lightly coat the cutlet on both sides with vegetable oil spray, set it aside, and continue dipping and coating the remaining cutlets in the same way.
5. Set the cutlets in the basket and air-fry undisturbed for 10 minutes, or until crisp and brown. Use kitchen tongs to transfer the cutlets to a wire rack to cool for a few minutes.
6. Meanwhile, stir the cranberry sauce with the cinnamon and ginger in a small bowl. Mix the shredded Brussels sprouts and mayonnaise in a second bowl until the vegetable is evenly coated.
7. Build the sandwiches by spreading about 1½ tablespoons of the cranberry mixture on the cut side of the bottom half of each roll. Set a cutlet on top, then spread about 3 tablespoons of the Brussels sprouts mixture evenly over the cutlet. Set the other half of the roll on top and serve warm.

### Variations & Ingredients Tips:

- Use leftover roasted turkey instead of turkey cutlets for a post-Thanksgiving sandwich.
- Substitute Brussels sprouts with shredded cabbage or kale for a different texture and flavor.
- Add a slice of brie or provolone cheese to the sandwich for extra creaminess.

**Per Serving:** Calories: 530; Cholesterol: 75mg; Total Fat: 22g; Saturated Fat: 4g; Sodium: 1180mg; Total Carbohydrates: 53g; Dietary Fiber: 4g; Total Sugars: 15g; Protein: 33g

## Chicken Gyros

**Servings: 4 | Prep Time: 10 Minutes (plus Marinating Time) | Cooking Time: 14 Minutes**

### Ingredients:

- 4 110 to 140-gram boneless skinless chicken thighs, trimmed of any fat blobs
- 2 tablespoons Lemon juice
- 2 tablespoons Red wine vinegar
- 2 tablespoons Olive oil
- 2 teaspoons Dried oregano
- 2 teaspoons Minced garlic
- 1 teaspoon Table salt
- 1 teaspoon Ground black pepper
- 4 Pita pockets (gluten-free, if a concern)
- ½ cup Chopped tomatoes
- ½ cup Bottled regular, low-fat, or fat-free ranch dressing (gluten-free, if a concern)

### Directions:

1. Mix the thighs, lemon juice, vinegar, oil, oregano, garlic, salt, and pepper in a zip-closed bag. Seal, gently massage the marinade into the meat through the plastic, and refrigerate for at least 2 hours or up to 6 hours. (Longer than that and the meat can turn rubbery.)
2. Set the plastic bag out on the counter (to make the contents a little less frigid). Preheat the air fryer to 190°C/375°F.
3. When the machine is at temperature, use kitchen tongs to place the thighs in the basket in one layer. Discard the marinade. Air-fry the chicken thighs undisturbed for 12 minutes, or until browned and an instant-read meat thermometer inserted into the thickest part of one thigh registers 75°C/165°F. You may need to air-fry the chicken 2 minutes longer if the machine's temperature is 70°C/360°F.
4. Use kitchen tongs to transfer the thighs to a cutting board. Cool for 5 minutes, then set one thigh in each of the pita pockets. Top each with 2 tablespoons chopped tomatoes and 2 tablespoons dressing. Serve warm.

### Variations & Ingredients Tips:

- Substitute chicken thighs with chicken breast for a leaner option.
- Add shredded lettuce, sliced onions, or cucumbers for extra crunch and flavor.
- Use homemade tzatziki sauce instead of ranch dressing for a more authentic taste.

**Per Serving:** Calories: 460; Cholesterol: 95mg; Total Fat: 28g; Saturated Fat: 5g; Sodium: 1070mg; Total Carbohydrates: 29g; Dietary Fiber: 2g; Total Sugars: 4g; Protein: 25g

## Mexican Cheeseburgers

**Servings: 4 | Prep Time: 20 Minutes | Cooking Time: 22 Minutes**

### Ingredients:

- 570 grams ground beef
- ¼ cup finely chopped onion
- ½ cup crushed yellow corn tortilla chips
- 1 (35-gram) packet taco seasoning
- ¼ cup canned diced green chilies
- 1 egg, lightly beaten
- 115 grams pepper jack cheese, grated
- 4 (30-cm) flour tortillas
- shredded lettuce, sour cream, guacamole, salsa (for topping)

### Directions:

1. Combine the ground beef, minced onion, crushed tortilla chips, taco seasoning, green chilies, and egg in a large bowl. Mix thoroughly until combined – your hands are good tools for this. Divide the meat into four equal portions and shape each portion into an oval-shaped burger.
2. Preheat the air fryer to 190°C/370°F.
3. Air-fry the burgers for 18 minutes, turning them over halfway through the cooking time. Divide the cheese between the burgers, lower fryer to 170°C/340°F and air-fry for an additional 4 minutes to melt the cheese. (This will give you a burger that is medium-well. If you prefer your cheeseburger medium-rare, shorten the cooking time to about 15 minutes and then add the cheese and proceed with the recipe.)
4. While the burgers are cooking, warm the tortillas wrapped in aluminum foil in a 175°C/350°F oven, or in a skillet with a little oil over medium-high heat for a couple of minutes. Keep the tortillas warm until the burgers are ready.
5. To assemble the burgers, spread sour cream over three quarters of the tortillas and top each with some shredded lettuce and salsa. Place the Mexican cheeseburgers on the lettuce and top with guacamole. Fold the tortillas around the burger, starting with the bottom and then folding the sides in over the top. (A little sour cream can help hold the seam of the tortilla together.) Serve immediately.

### Variations & Ingredients Tips:

- Use ground turkey or chicken for a leaner burger option.
- Substitute pepper jack cheese with Monterey Jack or cheddar cheese if preferred.
- Add sliced jalapeños or hot sauce to the burger mixture for extra heat.

**Per Serving (1 burger):** Calories: 780; Cholesterol: 165mg; Total Fat: 44g; Saturated Fat: 18g; Sodium: 1480mg; Total Carbohydrates: 51g; Dietary Fiber: 4g; Total Sugars: 4g; Protein: 46g

## Dijon Thyme Burgers

**Servings: 3 | Prep Time: 15 Minutes | Cooking Time: 18 Minutes**

### Ingredients:

- 450 grams lean ground beef
- ⅓ cup panko breadcrumbs
- ¼ cup finely chopped onion
- 3 tablespoons Dijon mustard
- 1 tablespoon chopped fresh thyme
- 4 teaspoons Worcestershire sauce
- 1 teaspoon salt
- freshly ground black pepper
- Topping (optional):
- 2 tablespoons Dijon mustard
- 1 tablespoon dark brown sugar
- 1 teaspoon Worcestershire sauce
- 115 grams sliced Swiss cheese, optional

### Directions:

1. Combine all the burger ingredients together in a large bowl and mix well. Divide the meat into 4 equal portions and then form the burgers, being careful not to over-handle the meat. One good way to do this is to throw the meat back and forth from one hand to another, packing the meat each time you catch it. Flatten the balls into patties, making an indentation in the center of each patty with your thumb (this will help it stay flat as it cooks) and flattening the sides of the burgers so that they will fit nicely into the air fryer basket.
2. Preheat the air fryer to 190°C/370°F.
3. If you don't have room for all four burgers, air-fry two or three burgers at a time for 8 minutes. Flip the burgers over and air-fry for another 6 minutes.
4. While the burgers are cooking combine the Dijon mustard, dark brown sugar, and Worcestershire sauce in a small bowl and mix well. This optional topping to the burgers really adds a boost of flavor at the end. Spread the Dijon topping evenly on each burger. If you cooked the burgers in batches, return the first batch to the cooker at this time – it's ok to place the fourth burger on top of the others in the center of the basket. Air-fry the burgers for another 3 minutes.
5. Finally, if desired, top each burger with a slice of Swiss cheese. Lower the air fryer temperature to 165°C/330°F and air-fry for another minute to melt the cheese. Serve the burgers on toasted brioche buns, dressed the way you like them.

### Variations & Ingredients Tips:

- Use ground turkey or chicken for a leaner burger option.
- Add minced garlic or finely chopped herbs like parsley or chives for extra flavor.
- Substitute panko breadcrumbs with regular breadcrumbs or oats for a different texture.

**Per Serving (1 burger with cheese):** Calories: 500; Cholesterol: 120mg; Total Fat: 27g; Saturated Fat: 11g; Sodium: 1180mg; Total Carbohydrates: 21g; Dietary Fiber: 1g; Total Sugars: 5g; Protein: 41g

## White Bean Veggie Burgers

**Servings: 3 | Prep Time: 15 Minutes | Cooking Time: 13 Minutes**

### Ingredients:

- 320 grams Drained and rinsed canned white beans
- 3 tablespoons Rolled oats (not quick-cooking or steel-cut; gluten-free, if a concern)
- 3 tablespoons Chopped walnuts
- 2 teaspoons Olive oil
- 2 teaspoons Lemon juice
- 1½ teaspoons Dijon mustard (gluten-free, if a concern)
- ¾ teaspoon Dried sage leaves
- ¼ teaspoon Table salt
- Olive oil spray
- 3 Whole-wheat buns or gluten-free whole-grain buns (if a concern), split open

### Directions:

1. Preheat the air fryer to 200°C/400°F.
2. Place the beans, oats, walnuts, oil, lemon juice, mustard, sage, and salt in a food processor. Cover and process to make a coarse paste that will hold its shape, about like wet sugar-cookie dough, stopping the machine to scrape down the inside of the canister at least once.
3. Scrape down and remove the blade. With clean and wet hands, form the bean paste into two 10-cm patties for the small batch, three 10-cm patties for the medium, or four 10-cm patties for the large batch. Generously coat the patties on both sides with olive oil spray.
4. Set them in the basket with some space between them and air-fry undisturbed for 12 minutes, or until lightly brown and crisp at the edges. The tops of the burgers will feel firm to the touch.
5. Use a nonstick-safe spatula, and perhaps a flatware fork for balance, to transfer the burgers to a cutting board. Set the buns cut side down in the basket in one layer (working in batches as necessary) and air-fry undisturbed for 1 minute, to toast a bit and warm up. Serve the burgers warm in the buns.

### Variations & Ingredients Tips:

- Use black beans, chickpeas, or lentils instead of white beans for a different flavor and color.
- Add grated carrots, zucchini, or beets to the burger mixture for extra nutrition and texture.
- Serve with your favorite burger toppings like lettuce, tomato, onion, and pickles.

**Per Serving (1 burger):** Calories: 350; Cholesterol: 0mg; Total Fat: 13g; Saturated Fat: 1g; Sodium: 520mg; Total Carbohydrates: 48g; Dietary Fiber: 9g; Total Sugars: 4g; Protein: 14g

## Black Bean Veggie Burgers

**Servings: 3 | Prep Time: 15 Minutes | Cooking Time: 10 Minutes**

### Ingredients:

- 1 cup Drained and rinsed canned black beans
- ⅓ cup Pecan pieces
- ⅓ cup Rolled oats (not quick-cooking or steel-cut; gluten-free, if a concern)
- 2 tablespoons (or 1 small egg) Pasteurized egg substitute, such as Egg Beaters (gluten-free, if a concern)
- 2 teaspoons Red ketchup-like chili sauce, such as Heinz
- ¼ teaspoon Ground cumin
- ¼ teaspoon Dried oregano
- ¼ teaspoon Table salt
- ¼ teaspoon Ground black pepper
- Olive oil
- Olive oil spray

### Directions:

1. Preheat the air fryer to 200°C/400°F.
2. Put the beans, pecans, oats, egg substitute or egg, chili sauce, cumin, oregano, salt, and pepper in a food processor. Cover and process to a coarse paste that will hold its shape like sugar-cookie dough, adding olive oil in 1-teaspoon increments to get the mixture to blend smoothly. The amount of olive oil is actually dependent on the internal moisture content of the beans and the oats. Figure on about 1 tablespoon (three 1-teaspoon additions) for the smaller batch, with proportional increases for the other batches. A little too much olive oil can't hurt, but a dry paste will fall apart as it cooks and a far-too-wet paste will stick to the basket.
3. Scrape down and remove the blade. Using clean, wet hands, form the paste into two 10 cm patties for the small batch, three 10 cm patties for the medium, or four 10 cm patties for the large batch, setting them one by one on a cutting board. Generously coat both sides of the patties with olive oil spray.
4. Set them in the basket in one layer. Air-fry undisturbed for 10 minutes, or until lightly browned and crisp at the edges.
5. Use a nonstick-safe spatula, and perhaps a flatware fork for balance, to transfer the burgers to a wire rack. Cool for 5 minutes before serving.

### Variations & Ingredients Tips:

- Add finely chopped vegetables like bell peppers, onions, or carrots for extra flavor and nutrition.
- Experiment with different spices and herbs, such as smoked paprika, garlic powder, or cilantro.
- For a gluten-free version, ensure all ingredients are certified gluten-free.

**Per Serving:** Calories: 280; Cholesterol: 0mg; Total Fat: 15g; Saturated Fat: 2g; Sodium: 420mg; Total Carbohydrates: 28g; Dietary Fiber: 8g; Total Sugars: 2g; Protein: 10g

## Perfect Burgers

**Servings: 3 | Prep Time: 10 Minutes | Cooking Time: 13 Minutes**

### Ingredients:

- 510 grams 90% lean ground beef
- 1½ tablespoons Worcestershire sauce (gluten-free, if a concern)
- ½ teaspoon Ground black pepper
- 3 Hamburger buns (gluten-free if a concern), split open

### Directions:

1. Preheat the air fryer to 190°C/375°F.
2. Gently mix the ground beef, Worcestershire sauce, and pepper in a bowl until well combined but preserving as much of the meat's fibers as possible. Divide this mixture into two 15-cm patties for the small batch, three 12.5-cm patties for the medium, or four 12.5-cm patties for the large. Make a thumbprint indentation in the center of each patty, about halfway through the meat.
3. Set the patties in the basket in one layer with some space between them. Air-fry undisturbed for 10 minutes, or until an instant-read meat thermometer inserted into the center of a burger registers 70°C/160°F (a medium-well burger). You may need to add 2 minutes cooking time if the air fryer is at 180°C/360°F.
4. Use a nonstick-safe spatula, and perhaps a flatware fork for balance, to transfer the burgers to a cutting board. Set the buns cut side down in the basket in one layer (working in batches as necessary) and air-fry undisturbed for 1 minute, to toast a bit and warm up. Serve the burgers in the warm buns.

### Variations & Ingredients Tips:

- Mix in finely chopped onions, garlic, or herbs to the burger mixture for extra flavor.
- Use a mixture of ground beef and ground pork or lamb for a juicier, more flavorful burger.
- Top burgers with your favorite cheese, bacon, avocado, or sautéed mushrooms.

**Per Serving (1 burger):** Calories: 420; Cholesterol: 105mg; Total Fat: 22g; Saturated Fat: 8g; Sodium: 460mg; Total Carbohydrates: 23g; Dietary Fiber: 1g; Total Sugars: 3g; Protein: 34g

## Sausage And Pepper Heros

**Servings: 3 | Prep Time: 10 Minutes | Cooking Time: 11 Minutes**

### Ingredients:

- 3 links (about 255 grams total) Sweet Italian sausages (gluten-free, if a concern)
- 1½ Medium red or green bell pepper(s), stemmed, cored, and cut into 1.25-cm-wide strips
- 1 medium Yellow or white onion(s), peeled, halved, and sliced into thin half-moons
- 3 Long soft rolls, such as hero, hoagie, or Italian sub rolls (gluten-free, if a concern), split open lengthwise
- For garnishing Balsamic vinegar
- For garnishing Fresh basil leaves

### Directions:

1. Preheat the air fryer to 200°C/400°F.
2. When the machine is at temperature, set the sausage links in the basket in one layer and air-fry undisturbed for 5 minutes.
3. Add the pepper strips and onions. Continue air-frying, tossing and rearranging everything about once every minute, for 5 minutes, or until the sausages are browned and an instant-read meat thermometer inserted into one of the links registers 70°C/160°F.
4. Use a nonstick-safe spatula and kitchen tongs to transfer the sausages and vegetables to a cutting board. Set the rolls cut side down in the basket in one layer (working in batches as necessary) and air-fry undisturbed for 1 minute, to toast the rolls a bit and warm them up. Set 1 sausage with some pepper strips and onions in each warm roll, sprinkle balsamic vinegar over the sandwich fillings, and garnish with basil leaves.

### Variations & Ingredients Tips:

- Use hot Italian sausage or chorizo for a spicier sandwich.
- Add sliced mushrooms or zucchini to the pepper and onion mixture for extra veggies.
- Top with shredded mozzarella or provolone cheese for a cheesy twist.

**Per Serving (1 sandwich):** Calories: 560; Cholesterol: 60mg; Total Fat: 36g; Saturated Fat: 12g; Sodium: 1420mg; Total Carbohydrates: 39g; Dietary Fiber: 3g; Total Sugars: 7g; Protein: 24g

## Crunchy Falafel Balls

**Servings: 8 | Prep Time: 15 Minutes | Cooking Time: 16 Minutes**

### Ingredients:

- 600 grams Drained and rinsed canned chickpeas
- 60 grams Olive oil
- 3 tablespoons All-purpose flour
- 1½ teaspoons Dried oregano
- 1½ teaspoons Dried sage leaves
- 1½ teaspoons Dried thyme
- ¾ teaspoon Table salt
- Olive oil spray

### Directions:

1. Preheat the air fryer to 200°C/400°F.
2. Place the chickpeas, olive oil, flour, oregano, sage, thyme, and salt in a food processor. Cover and process into a paste, stopping the machine at least once to scrape down the inside of the canister.
3. Scrape down and remove the blade. Using clean, wet hands, form 2 tablespoons of the paste into a ball, then continue making 9 more balls for a small batch, 15 more for a medium one, and 19 more for a large batch. Generously coat the balls in olive oil spray.
4. Set the balls in the basket in one layer with a little space between them and air-fry undisturbed for 16 minutes, or until well browned and crisp.
5. Dump the contents of the basket onto a wire rack. Cool for 5 minutes before serving.

### Variations & Ingredients Tips:

- Add minced garlic, onion, or herbs like parsley or cilantro for extra flavor.
- Serve with tahini sauce, hummus, or tzatziki for dipping.
- Make a falafel sandwich by stuffing pita bread with falafel balls, lettuce, tomato, and sauce.

**Per Serving (2 falafel balls):** Calories: 170; Cholesterol: 0mg; Total Fat: 9g; Saturated Fat: 1g; Sodium: 230mg; Total Carbohydrates: 18g; Dietary Fiber: 4g; Total Sugars: 2g; Protein: 5g

## Chicken Club Sandwiches

**Servings: 3 | Prep Time: 15 Minutes | Cooking Time: 15 Minutes**

### Ingredients:

- 3 140- to 170-gram boneless skinless chicken breasts
- 6 Thick-cut bacon strips (gluten-free, if a concern)
- 3 Long soft rolls, such as hero, hoagie, or Italian sub rolls (gluten-free, if a concern)
- 3 tablespoons Regular, low-fat, or fat-free mayonnaise (gluten-free, if a concern)
- 3 Lettuce leaves, preferably romaine or iceberg
- 6 6-mm-thick tomato slices

### Directions:

1. Preheat the air fryer to 190°C/375°F.
2. Wrap each chicken breast with 2 strips of bacon, spiraling the bacon around the meat, slightly overlapping the strips on each revolution. Start the second strip of bacon farther down the breast but on a line with the start of the first strip so they both end at a lined-up point on the chicken breast.
3. When the machine is at temperature, set the wrapped breasts bacon-seam side down in the basket with space between them. Air-fry undisturbed for 12 minutes, until the bacon is browned, crisp, and cooked through and an instant-read meat thermometer inserted into the center of a breast registers 75°C/165°F. You may need to add 2 minutes in the air fryer if the temperature is at 70°C/160°F.
4. Use kitchen tongs to transfer the breasts to a wire rack. Split the rolls open lengthwise and set them cut side down in the basket. Air-fry for 1 minute, or until warmed through.
5. Use kitchen tongs to transfer the rolls to a cutting board. Spread 1 tablespoon mayonnaise on the cut side of one half of each roll. Top with a chicken breast, lettuce leaf, and tomato slice. Serve warm.

### Variations & Ingredients Tips:

- Use turkey bacon for a lower-fat option.
- Add sliced avocado or pickled onions for extra flavor and texture.
- Toast the rolls before assembling the sandwiches for a crispy texture.

**Per Serving:** Calories: 640; Cholesterol: 110mg; Total Fat: 34g; Saturated Fat: 9g; Sodium: 1180mg; Total Carbohydrates: 44g; Dietary Fiber: 2g; Total Sugars: 5g; Protein: 42g

## Inside Out Cheeseburgers

**Servings: 2 | Prep Time: 15 Minutes | Cooking Time: 20 Minutes**

### Ingredients:

- 340 grams lean ground beef
- 3 tablespoons minced onion
- 4 teaspoons ketchup
- 2 teaspoons yellow mustard
- salt and freshly ground black pepper
- 4 slices of Cheddar cheese, broken into smaller pieces
- 8 hamburger dill pickle chips

### Directions:

1. Combine the ground beef, minced onion, ketchup, mustard, salt and pepper in a large bowl. Mix well to thoroughly combine the ingredients. Divide the meat into four equal portions.
2. To make the stuffed burgers, flatten each portion of meat into a thin patty. Place 4 pickle chips and half of the cheese onto the center of two of the patties, leaving a rim around the edge of the patty exposed. Place the remaining two patties on top of the first and press the meat together firmly, sealing the edges tightly. With the burgers on a flat surface, press the sides of the burger with the palm of your hand to create a straight edge. This will help keep the stuffing inside the burger while it cooks.
3. Preheat the air fryer to 190°C/370°F.
4. Place the burgers inside the air fryer basket and air-fry for 20 minutes, flipping the burgers over halfway through the cooking time.
5. Serve the cheeseburgers on buns with lettuce and tomato.

### Variations & Ingredients Tips:

- Use different types of cheese like Swiss, pepper jack, or blue cheese for a unique flavor.
- Add crispy bacon pieces or sautéed mushrooms to the stuffing for extra richness.
- Brush the burgers with a mixture of melted butter and minced garlic before cooking for added flavor.

**Per Serving (1 burger):** Calories: 510; Cholesterol: 145mg; Total Fat: 32g; Saturated Fat: 14g; Sodium: 780mg; Total Carbohydrates: 12g; Dietary Fiber: 1g; Total Sugars: 6g; Protein: 42g

## Philly Cheesesteak Sandwiches

**Servings: 3 | Prep Time: 10 Minutes | Cooking Time: 9 Minutes**

### Ingredients:

- 340 grams Shaved beef
- 1 tablespoon Worcestershire sauce (gluten-free, if a concern)
- ¼ teaspoon Garlic powder
- ¼ teaspoon Mild paprika
- 6 tablespoons (45 grams) Frozen bell pepper strips (do not thaw)
- 2 slices, broken into rings Very thin yellow or white medium onion slice(s)
- 170 grams (6 to 8 slices) Provolone cheese slices
- 3 Long soft rolls such as hero, hoagie, or Italian sub rolls, or hot dog buns (gluten-free, if a concern), split open lengthwise

### Directions:

1. Preheat the air fryer to 200°C/400°F.
2. When the machine is at temperature, spread the shaved beef in the basket, leaving a 1.25-cm perimeter around the meat for good air flow. Sprinkle the meat with the Worcestershire sauce, paprika, and garlic powder. Spread the peppers and onions on top of the meat.
3. Air-fry undisturbed for 6 minutes, or until cooked through. Set the cheese on top of the meat. Continue air-frying undisturbed for 3 minutes, or until the cheese has melted.
4. Use kitchen tongs to divide the meat and cheese layers in the basket between the rolls or buns. Serve hot.

### Variations & Ingredients Tips:

- Use thinly sliced ribeye or sirloin steak instead of shaved beef for a more traditional texture.
- Add sliced mushrooms to the pepper and onion mixture for extra flavor and nutrition.
- Substitute provolone with American cheese or Cheez Whiz for a classic Philly taste.

**Per Serving:** Calories: 620; Cholesterol: 135mg; Total Fat: 32g; Saturated Fat: 15g; Sodium: 1320mg; Total Carbohydrates: 38g; Dietary Fiber: 2g; Total Sugars: 5g; Protein: 48g

## Chicken Saltimbocca Sandwiches

**Servings: 3 | Prep Time: 10 Minutes | Cooking Time: 11 Minutes**

### Ingredients:

- 3 140to 170-gram boneless skinless chicken breasts
- 6 Thin prosciutto slices
- 6 Provolone cheese slices
- 3 Long soft rolls, such as hero, hoagie, or Italian sub rolls (gluten-free, if a concern), split open lengthwise
- 3 tablespoons Pesto, purchased or homemade (see the headnote)

### Directions:

1. Preheat the air fryer to 200°C/400°F.
2. Wrap each chicken breast with 2 prosciutto slices, spiraling the prosciutto around the breast and overlapping the slices a bit to cover the breast. The prosciutto will stick to the chicken more readily than bacon does.
3. When the machine is at temperature, set the wrapped chicken breasts in the basket and air-fry undisturbed for 10 minutes, or until the prosciutto is frizzled and the chicken is cooked through.
4. Overlap 2 cheese slices on each breast. Air-fry undisturbed for 1 minute, or until melted. Take the basket out of the machine.
5. Smear the insides of the rolls with the pesto, then use kitchen tongs to put a wrapped and cheesy chicken breast in each roll.

### Variations & Ingredients Tips:

- Use fresh mozzarella instead of provolone for a creamier texture.
- Add sliced tomatoes or roasted red peppers for extra flavor and nutrition.
- Substitute prosciutto with ham or bacon if desired.

**Per Serving:** Calories: 630; Cholesterol: 125mg; Total Fat: 32g; Saturated Fat: 11g; Sodium: 1580mg; Total Carbohydrates: 38g; Dietary Fiber: 2g; Total Sugars: 4g; Protein: 48g

## Inside-out Cheeseburgers

**Servings: 3 | Prep Time: 15 Minutes | Cooking Time: 9-11 Minutes**

### Ingredients:

- 510 grams 90% lean ground beef
- ¾ teaspoon Dried oregano
- ¾ teaspoon Table salt
- ¾ teaspoon Ground black pepper
- ¼ teaspoon Garlic powder
- 6 tablespoons (about 45 grams) Shredded Cheddar, Swiss, or other semi-firm cheese, or a purchased blend of

shredded cheeses
- 3 Hamburger buns (gluten-free, if a concern), split open

### Directions:

1. Preheat the air fryer to 190°C/375°F.
2. Gently mix the ground beef, oregano, salt, pepper, and garlic powder in a bowl until well combined without turning the mixture to mush. Form it into two 15-cm patties for the small batch, three for the medium, or four for the large.
3. Place 2 tablespoons of the shredded cheese in the center of each patty. With clean hands, fold the sides of the patty up to cover the cheese, then pick it up and roll it gently into a ball to seal the cheese inside. Gently press it back into a 12.5-cm burger without letting any cheese squish out. Continue filling and preparing more burgers, as needed.
4. Place the burgers in the basket in one layer and air-fry undisturbed for 8 minutes for medium or 10 minutes for well-done. (An instant-read meat thermometer won't work for these burgers because it will hit the mostly melted cheese inside and offer a hotter temperature than the surrounding meat.)
5. Use a nonstick-safe spatula, and perhaps a flatware fork for balance, to transfer the burgers to a cutting board. Set the buns cut side down in the basket in one layer (working in batches as necessary) and air-fry undisturbed for 1 minute, to toast a bit and warm up. Cool the burgers a few minutes more, then serve them warm in the buns.

### Variations & Ingredients Tips:

- Mix different types of cheese like cheddar, mozzarella, and blue cheese for a flavorful combination.
- Add finely chopped bacon or caramelized onions to the cheese stuffing for extra richness.
- Serve with your favorite burger toppings like lettuce, tomato, onion, and pickles.

**Per Serving (1 burger):** Calories: 480; Cholesterol: 125mg; Total Fat: 27g; Saturated Fat: 11g; Sodium: 720mg; Total Carbohydrates: 22g; Dietary Fiber: 1g; Total Sugars: 3g; Protein: 38g

# Vegetarian Recipes

## Party Giant Nachos

**Servings: 2 | Prep Time: 10 Minutes | Cooking Time: 20 Minutes**

### Ingredients:

- 2 tbsp sour cream
- ½ tsp chili powder
- Salt to taste
- 2 soft corn tortillas
- 2 tsp avocado oil
- ½ cup refried beans
- ¼ cup cheddar cheese shreds
- 2 tbsp Parmesan cheese
- 2 tbsp sliced black olives
- ¼ cup torn iceberg lettuce
- ¼ cup baby spinach
- ½ sliced avocado
- 1 tomato, diced
- 2 lime wedges

### Directions:

1. Preheat air fryer at 200°C/400°F.
2. Whisk the sour cream, chili powder, and salt in a small bowl.
3. Brush tortillas with avocado oil and season one side with salt. Place tortillas in the air fryer basket and Bake for 3 minutes. Set aside.
4. Layer the refried beans, Parmesan and cheddar cheeses in the tortillas. Place them back into the basket and Bake for 2 minutes.
5. Divide tortillas into 2 serving plates. Top each tortilla with black olives, baby spinach, lettuce, and tomatoes. Dollop sour cream mixture on each.
6. Serve with lime and avocado wedges on the side.

### Variations & Ingredients Tips:

- Add sliced jalapeños or hot sauce for a spicy kick.
- Use Greek yogurt instead of sour cream for a healthier option.
- Substitute refried beans with black beans or pinto beans.

**Per Serving:** Calories: 380; Total Fat: 24g; Saturated Fat: 7g; Sodium: 780mg; Total Carbohydrates: 32g; Dietary Fiber: 9g; Total Sugars: 5g; Protein: 13g

## Black Bean Stuffed Potato Boats

**Servings: 4 | Prep Time: 15 Minutes | Cooking Time: 55 Minutes**

### Ingredients:

- 4 russets potatoes
- 1 cup chipotle mayonnaise
- 1 cup canned black beans
- 2 tomatoes, chopped
- 1 scallion, chopped
- 1/3 cup chopped cilantro
- 1 poblano chile, minced
- 1 avocado, diced

**Directions:**

1. Preheat air fryer to 200°C/390°F. Clean the potatoes, poke with a fork, and spray with oil. Put in the air fryer and Bake for 30 minutes or until softened.
2. Heat the beans in a pan over medium heat. Put the potatoes on a plate and cut them across the top. Open them with a fork so you can stuff them. Top each potato with chipotle mayonnaise, beans, tomatoes, scallions, cilantro, poblano chile, and avocado. Serve immediately.

**Variations & Ingredients Tips:**

- Substitute black beans with refried beans or lentils for a different protein option.
- Use sour cream or Greek yogurt instead of chipotle mayonnaise for a milder flavor.
- Add shredded cheese, salsa, or pickled jalapeños for extra toppings.

**Per Serving (1 potato):** Calories: 490; Cholesterol: 15mg; Total Fat: 33g; Saturated Fat: 5g; Sodium: 670mg; Total Carbohydrates: 46g; Dietary Fiber: 9g; Total Sugars: 6g; Protein: 9g

## Creamy Broccoli & Mushroom Casserole

**Servings: 4 | Prep Time: 10 Minutes | Cooking Time: 30 Minutes**

**Ingredients:**

- 4 cups broccoli florets, chopped
- 1 cup crushed cheddar cheese crisps
- 1/4 cup diced onion
- 1/4 tsp dried thyme
- 1/4 tsp dried marjoram
- 1/4 tsp dried oregano
- 1/2 cup diced mushrooms
- 1 egg
- 2 tbsp sour cream
- 1/4 cup mayonnaise
- Salt and pepper to taste

**Directions:**

1. Preheat air fryer to 175°C/350°F.
2. Combine all ingredients, except for the cheese crisps, in a bowl.
3. Spoon mixture into a round cake pan. Place cake pan in the frying basket and Bake for 14 minutes.
4. Let sit for 10 minutes. Distribute crushed cheddar cheese crisps over the top and serve.

**Variations & Ingredients Tips:**

- Add cooked bacon or ham for extra protein and flavor.
- Substitute sour cream with Greek yogurt for a tangy twist.
- Top with breadcrumbs or crushed crackers before baking for a crispy topping.

**Per Serving:** Calories: 210; Total Fat: 15g; Saturated Fat: 5g; Cholesterol: 55mg; Sodium: 330mg; Total Carbs: 13g; Dietary Fiber: 4g; Total Sugars: 3g; Protein: 8g

## Thyme Lentil Patties

**Servings: 2 | Prep Time: 15 Minutes | Cooking Time: 35 Minutes**

**Ingredients:**

- ½ cup grated American cheese
- 1 cup cooked lentils
- ¼ tsp dried thyme
- 2 eggs, beaten
- Salt and pepper to taste
- 1 cup bread crumbs

**Directions:**

1. Preheat air fryer to 180°C/350°F.
2. Put the eggs, lentils, and cheese in a bowl and mix to combine. Stir in half the bread crumbs, thyme, salt, and pepper.
3. Form the mixture into 2 patties and coat them in the remaining bread crumbs.
4. Transfer to the greased air fryer basket. Air Fry for 14-16 minutes until brown, flipping once.
5. Serve.

**Variations & Ingredients Tips:**

- Use Swiss, cheddar, or mozzarella cheese instead of American.
- Add finely chopped onions, garlic, or bell peppers to the mixture.
- Serve on a bun with lettuce, tomato, and mayonnaise.

**Per Serving:** Calories: 470; Total Fat: 16g; Saturated Fat: 8g; Sodium: 960mg; Total Carbohydrates: 56g; Dietary Fiber: 12g; Total Sugars: 4g; Protein: 30g

## Asparagus, Mushroom And Cheese Soufflés

**Servings: 3 | Prep Time: 20 Minutes | Cooking Time: 21 Minutes**

**Ingredients:**

- butter
- grated Parmesan cheese
- 3 button mushrooms, thinly sliced
- 8 spears asparagus, sliced 1.25-cm long
- 1 teaspoon olive oil
- 1 tablespoon butter
- 4½ teaspoons flour
- pinch paprika
- pinch ground nutmeg
- salt and freshly ground black pepper
- ½ cup milk
- ½ cup grated Gruyère cheese or other Swiss cheese
- 2 eggs, separated

**Directions:**

1. Butter three 170-g ramekins and dust with grated Parmesan

cheese. (Butter the ramekins and then coat the butter with Parmesan by shaking it around in the ramekin and dumping out any excess.)
2. Preheat the air fryer to 200°C/400°F.
3. Toss the mushrooms and asparagus in a bowl with the olive oil. Transfer the vegetables to the air fryer and air-fry for 7 minutes, shaking the basket once or twice to redistribute the ingredients while they cook.
4. While the vegetables are cooking, make the soufflé base. Melt the butter in a saucepan on the stovetop over medium heat. Add the flour, stir and cook for a minute or two. Add the paprika, nutmeg, salt and pepper. Whisk in the milk and bring the mixture to a simmer to thicken. Remove the pan from the heat and add the cheese, stirring to melt. Let the mixture cool for just a few minutes and then whisk the egg yolks in, one at a time. Stir in the cooked mushrooms and asparagus. Let this soufflé base cool.
5. In a separate bowl, whisk the egg whites to soft peak stage (the point at which the whites can almost stand up on the end of your whisk). Fold the whipped egg whites into the soufflé base, adding a little at a time.
6. Preheat the air fryer to 165°C/330°F.
7. Transfer the batter carefully to the buttered ramekins, leaving about 1.25-cm at the top. Place the ramekins into the air fryer basket and air-fry for 14 minutes. The soufflés should have risen nicely and be brown on top. Serve immediately.

## Variations & Ingredients Tips:

- Use different vegetables like spinach, broccoli, or bell peppers for a variety of flavors.
- Substitute Gruyère with cheddar, gouda, or brie for a different cheese profile.
- Serve the soufflés with a side salad or crusty bread for a complete meal.

**Per Serving (1 soufflé):** Calories: 290; Cholesterol: 165mg; Total Fat: 20g; Saturated Fat: 11g; Sodium: 410mg; Total Carbohydrates: 12g; Dietary Fiber: 1g; Total Sugars: 4g; Protein: 16g

## Spicy Sesame Tempeh Slaw With Peanut Dressing

**Servings: 2 | Prep Time: 20 Minutes (plus Marinating Time) | Cooking Time: 8 Minutes**

### Ingredients:

- 2 cups hot water
- 1 teaspoon salt
- 227 grams tempeh, sliced into 2.5-cm-long pieces
- 2 tablespoons low-sodium soy sauce
- 2 tablespoons rice vinegar
- 1 tablespoon filtered water
- 2 teaspoons sesame oil
- ½ teaspoon fresh ginger
- 1 clove garlic, minced
- ¼ teaspoon black pepper
- ½ jalapeño, sliced
- 4 cups cabbage slaw
- 4 tablespoons Peanut Dressing (see the following recipe)
- 2 tablespoons fresh chopped cilantro
- 2 tablespoons chopped peanuts

### Directions:

1. Mix the hot water with the salt and pour over the tempeh in a glass bowl. Stir and cover with a towel for 10 minutes.
2. Discard the water and leave the tempeh in the bowl.
3. In a medium bowl, mix the soy sauce, rice vinegar, filtered water, sesame oil, ginger, garlic, pepper, and jalapeño. Pour over the tempeh and cover with a towel. Place in the refrigerator to marinate for at least 2 hours.
4. Preheat the air fryer to 190°C/370°F. Remove the tempeh from the bowl and discard the remaining marinade.
5. Liberally spray the metal trivet that goes into the air fryer basket and place the tempeh on top of the trivet.
6. Cook for 4 minutes, flip, and cook another 4 minutes.
7. In a large bowl, mix the cabbage slaw with the Peanut Dressing and toss in the cilantro and chopped peanuts.
8. Portion onto 4 plates and place the cooked tempeh on top when cooking completes. Serve immediately.

### Variations & Ingredients Tips:

- Use extra-firm tofu instead of tempeh for a different protein.
- Add shredded carrots, bell peppers, or edamame to the slaw.
- Substitute peanut dressing with a sesame-ginger dressing.

**Per Serving:** Calories: 380; Total Fat: 23g; Saturated Fat: 3.5g; Sodium: 1210mg; Total Carbohydrates: 29g; Dietary Fiber: 8g; Total Sugars: 8g; Protein: 22g

## Gorgeous Jalapeño Poppers

**Servings: 6 | Prep Time: 15 Minutes | Cooking Time: 25 Minutes**

### Ingredients:

- 6 center-cut bacon slices, halved
- 6 jalapeños, halved lengthwise
- 115g cream cheese
- 1/4 cup grated Gruyere cheese
- 2 tbsp chopped chives

### Directions:

1. Scoop out seeds and membranes of the jalapeño halves, discard.
2. Combine cream cheese, Gruyere cheese, and chives in a bowl.
3. Fill the jalapeño halves with the cream cheese filling using a small spoon.
4. Wrap each pepper with a slice of bacon and secure with a toothpick.
5. Preheat air fryer to 165°C/325°F.
6. Put the stuffed peppers in a single layer on the greased fry-

ing basket and Bake until the peppers are tender, cheese is melted, and the bacon is browned, 11-13 minutes.
7. Serve warm.

### Variations & Ingredients Tips:

- Use turkey bacon for a lighter option.
- Mix shredded cheddar into the cream cheese filling.
- Add a drizzle of ranch dressing when serving.

**Per Serving:** Calories: 180; Total Fat: 14g; Saturated Fat: 7g; Sodium: 330mg; Total Carbs: 4g; Dietary Fiber: 1g; Total Sugars: 2g; Protein: 9g

## Pinto Bean Casserole

**Servings: 2 | Prep Time: 5 Minutes | Cooking Time: 15 Minutes**

### Ingredients:

- 1 can pinto beans
- ¼ cup tomato sauce
- 2 tbsp cornstarch
- 2 garlic cloves, minced
- ½ tsp dried oregano
- ½ tsp cumin
- 1 tsp smoked paprika
- Salt and pepper to taste

### Directions:

1. Preheat air fryer to 200°C/390°F.
2. Stir the beans, tomato sauce, cornstarch, garlic, oregano, cumin, smoked paprika, salt, and pepper in a bowl until combined.
3. Pour the bean mix into a greased baking pan.
4. Bake in the fryer for 4 minutes. Remove, stir, and Bake for 4 minutes or until the mix is thick and heated through.
5. Serve hot.

### Variations & Ingredients Tips:

- Top with shredded cheese, sour cream, and chopped cilantro.
- Add diced bell peppers and onions for extra veggies.
- Use black beans or kidney beans for variation.

**Per Serving:** Calories: 280; Total Fat: 1.5g; Saturated Fat: 0g; Sodium: 980mg; Total Carbohydrates: 52g; Dietary Fiber: 15g; Total Sugars: 2g; Protein: 15g

## Roasted Vegetable Pita Pizza

**Servings: 4 | Prep Time: 10 Minutes | Cooking Time: 20 Minutes**

### Ingredients:

- 1 medium red bell pepper, seeded and cut into quarters
- 1 teaspoon extra-virgin olive oil
- ⅛ teaspoon black pepper
- ⅛ teaspoon salt
- Two 15-cm whole-grain pita breads
- 6 tablespoons pesto sauce
- ¼ small red onion, thinly sliced
- ½ cup shredded part-skim mozzarella cheese

### Directions:

1. Preheat the air fryer to 200°C/400°F.
2. In a small bowl, toss the bell peppers with the olive oil, pepper, and salt.
3. Place the bell peppers in the air fryer and cook for 15 minutes, shaking every 5 minutes to prevent burning.
4. Remove the peppers and set aside. Turn the air fryer temperature down to 180°C/350°F.
5. Lay the pita bread on a flat surface. Cover each with half the pesto sauce; then top with even portions of the red bell peppers and onions. Sprinkle cheese over the top. Spray the air fryer basket with olive oil mist.
6. Carefully lift the pita bread into the air fryer basket with a spatula.
7. Cook for 5 to 8 minutes, or until the outer edges begin to brown and the cheese is melted.
8. Serve warm with desired sides.

### Variations & Ingredients Tips:

- Use hummus or baba ganoush instead of pesto for a Mediterranean flavor.
- Add sliced mushrooms, zucchini, or eggplant for more veggie toppings.
- Sprinkle with red pepper flakes or dried oregano for extra seasoning.

**Per Serving:** Calories: 240; Total Fat: 12g; Saturated Fat: 3g; Sodium: 480mg; Total Carbohydrates: 26g; Dietary Fiber: 5g; Total Sugars: 4g; Protein: 10g

## Falafel

**Servings: 4 | Prep Time: 15 Minutes | Cooking Time: 10 Minutes**

### Ingredients:

- One 400-gram can garbanzo beans (chickpeas), drained and rinsed
- 1 clove garlic, chopped
- 1 cup chopped parsley
- ½ cup chopped dill
- ½ teaspoon ground cumin
- ½ teaspoon ground coriander
- 1 teaspoon salt
- ¼ cup sesame seeds
- ½ cup breadcrumbs

### Directions:

1. Preheat the air fryer to 175°C/350°F.
2. Pat the garbanzo beans dry with a towel. In a food processor, place the beans, garlic, parsley, dill, cumin, coriander, and salt. Blend for 2 minutes, scraping down the sides of the food processor every 30 seconds.
3. In a small bowl, mix together the breadcrumbs and sesa-

me seeds. Working one at a time and using a cookie scoop or approximately 2 tablespoons, form a patty about 1.25-cm thick and round. Dredge the patties in the breadcrumb mixture.

4. Place the falafel in the air fryer basket, making sure they don't overlap. Spray with cooking spray and cook for 6 minutes, flip over, and cook another 4 to 6 minutes. Cook in batches as needed.

### Variations & Ingredients Tips:

- Add diced onions, red pepper flakes, or lemon juice to the falafel mixture for extra flavor.
- Serve in a pita with lettuce, tomato, and tzatziki sauce for a classic falafel sandwich.
- Use a mixture of chickpeas and fava beans for a more authentic taste.

**Per Serving (3 falafel):** Calories: 250; Cholesterol: 0mg; Total Fat: 8g; Saturated Fat: 1g; Sodium: 770mg; Total Carbohydrates: 36g; Dietary Fiber: 8g; Total Sugars: 5g; Protein: 11g

## Roasted Veggie Bowls

**Servings: 4 | Prep Time: 10 Minutes | Cooking Time: 30 Minutes**

### Ingredients:

- 1 cup Brussels sprouts, trimmed and quartered
- ½ onion, cut into half-moons
- ½ cup green beans, chopped
- 1 cup broccoli florets
- 1 red bell pepper, sliced
- 1 yellow bell pepper, sliced
- 1 tbsp olive oil
- ½ tsp chili powder
- ¼ tsp ground cumin
- ¼ tsp ground coriander

### Directions:

1. Preheat air fryer to 180°C/350°F.
2. Combine all ingredients in a bowl.
3. Place veggie mixture in the air fryer basket and Air Fry for 15 minutes, tossing every 5 minutes.
4. Divide between 4 medium bowls and serve.

### Variations & Ingredients Tips:

- Add sweet potato chunks or butternut squash for a heartier bowl.
- Toss in canned chickpeas or black beans for added protein.
- Drizzle with tahini sauce or balsamic glaze before serving.

**Per Serving:** Calories: 100; Total Fat: 5g; Saturated Fat: 0.5g; Sodium: 35mg; Total Carbohydrates: 12g; Dietary Fiber: 4g; Total Sugars: 5g; Protein: 3g

## Rigatoni With Roasted Onions, Fennel, Spinach And Lemon Pepper Ricotta

**Servings: 2 | Prep Time: 10 Minutes | Cooking Time: 13 Minutes**

### Ingredients:

- 1 red onion, rough chopped into large chunks
- 2 teaspoons olive oil, divided
- 1 bulb fennel, sliced 0.6-cm thick
- ¾ cup ricotta cheese
- 1½ teaspoons finely chopped lemon zest, plus more for garnish
- 1 teaspoon lemon juice
- salt and freshly ground black pepper
- 227 grams dried rigatoni pasta
- 3 cups baby spinach leaves

### Directions:

1. Bring a large stockpot of salted water to a boil on the stovetop and Preheat the air fryer to 200°C/400°F.
2. While the water is coming to a boil, toss the chopped onion in 1 teaspoon of olive oil and transfer to the air fryer basket. Air-fry at 200°C/400°F for 5 minutes.
3. Toss the sliced fennel with 1 teaspoon of olive oil and add this to the air fryer basket with the onions. Continue to air-fry at 200°C/400°F for 8 minutes, shaking the basket a few times during the cooking process.
4. Combine the ricotta cheese, lemon zest and juice, ¼ teaspoon of salt and freshly ground black pepper in a bowl and stir until smooth.
5. Add the dried rigatoni to the boiling water and cook according to the package directions. When the pasta is cooked al dente, reserve one cup of the pasta water and drain the pasta into a colander.
6. Place the spinach in a serving bowl and immediately transfer the hot pasta to the bowl, wilting the spinach. Add the roasted onions and fennel and toss together. Add a little pasta water to the dish if it needs moistening. Then, dollop the lemon pepper ricotta cheese on top and nestle it into the hot pasta. Garnish with more lemon zest if desired.

### Variations & Ingredients Tips:

- Substitute fennel with sliced zucchini or eggplant.
- Use goat cheese or feta instead of ricotta for a tangy flavor.
- Add cooked chicken or shrimp for a non-vegetarian version.

**Per Serving:** Calories: 610; Total Fat: 19g; Saturated Fat: 9g; Sodium: 470mg; Total Carbohydrates: 89g; Dietary Fiber: 7g; Total Sugars: 8g; Protein: 24g

## Vietnamese Gingered Tofu

**Servings: 4 | Prep Time: 10 Minutes | Cooking Time: 25 Minutes**

### Ingredients:

- 1 package extra-firm tofu, cubed
- 4 tsp shoyu (soy sauce)
- 1 tsp onion powder
- 1/2 tsp garlic powder
- 1/2 tsp ginger powder
- 1/2 tsp turmeric powder
- Black pepper to taste
- 2 tbsp nutritional yeast
- 1 tsp dried rosemary
- 1 tsp dried dill
- 2 tsp cornstarch
- 2 tsp sunflower oil

### Directions:

1. Sprinkle the tofu with shoyu and toss to coat.
2. Add the onion, garlic, ginger, turmeric, and pepper. Gently toss to coat.
3. Add the yeast, rosemary, dill, and cornstarch. Toss to coat.
4. Dribble with the oil and toss again.
5. Preheat air fryer to 200°C/390°F. Spray the basket with oil.
6. Put the tofu in the basket and Bake for 7 minutes.
7. Remove, shake gently, and cook for another 7 minutes or until crispy and golden.
8. Serve warm.

### Variations & Ingredients Tips:

- Use tamari or coconut aminos instead of soy sauce.
- Add chili garlic sauce or sriracha for a spicy kick.
- Toss with chopped scallions before serving.

**Per Serving:** Calories: 132; Total Fat: 7g; Saturated Fat: 1g; Sodium: 514mg; Total Carbohydrates: 8g; Dietary Fiber: 2g; Total Sugars: 1g; Protein: 13g

## Vegetarian Paella

**Servings: 3 | Prep Time: 10 Minutes | Cooking Time: 50 Minutes**

### Ingredients:

- 1/2 cup chopped artichoke hearts
- 1/2 sliced red bell peppers
- 4 mushrooms, thinly sliced
- 1/2 cup canned diced tomatoes
- 1/2 cup canned chickpeas
- 3 tbsp hot sauce
- 2 tbsp lemon juice
- 1 tbsp allspice
- 1 cup rice

### Directions:

1. Preheat air fryer to 200°C/400°F.
2. Combine the artichokes, peppers, mushrooms, tomatoes and their juices, chickpeas, hot sauce, lemon juice, and allspice in a baking pan.
3. Roast for 10 minutes.
4. Pour in rice and 2 cups of boiling water, cover with aluminum foil, and Roast for 22 minutes.
5. Discard the foil and Roast for 3 minutes until the top is crisp.
6. Let cool slightly before stirring. Serve.

### Variations & Ingredients Tips:

- Use vegetable or mushroom broth instead of water.
- Add sliced vegan sausages or chickpea "shrimp".
- Garnish with lemon wedges and fresh parsley.

**Per Serving:** Calories: 320; Total Fat: 3g; Saturated Fat: 0g; Sodium: 768mg; Total Carbohydrates: 67g; Dietary Fiber: 8g; Total Sugars: 7g; Protein: 9g

## Pineapple & Veggie Souvlaki

**Servings: 4 | Prep Time: 20 Minutes | Cooking Time: 35 Minutes**

### Ingredients:

- 1 can pineapple rings in pineapple juice
- 1 red bell pepper, stemmed and seeded
- 1/3 cup butter
- 2 tbsp apple cider vinegar
- 2 tbsp hot sauce
- 1 tbsp allspice
- 1 tsp ground nutmeg
- 454 grams feta cheese
- 1 red onion, peeled
- 8 mushrooms, quartered

### Directions:

1. Preheat air fryer to 200°C/400°F.
2. Whisk the butter, pineapple juice, apple vinegar, hot sauce, allspice, and nutmeg until smooth. Set aside.
3. Slice feta cheese into 16 cubes, then the bell pepper into 16 chunks, and finally red onion into 8 wedges, separating each wedge into 2 pieces.
4. Cut pineapple ring into quarters. Place veggie cubes and feta into the butter bowl and toss to coat.
5. Thread the veggies, tofu, and pineapple onto 8 skewers, alternating 16 pieces on each skewer.
6. Grill for 15 minutes until golden brown and cooked. Serve warm.

### Variations & Ingredients Tips:

- Use halloumi cheese instead of feta for a firmer texture.
- Add zucchini, cherry tomatoes, or eggplant chunks to the skewers.
- Brush skewers with any leftover marinade during cooking for extra flavor.

**Per Serving:** Calories: 420; Total Fat: 33g; Saturated Fat: 21g; Sodium: 1120mg; Total Carbohydrates: 16g; Dietary Fiber: 2g; Total Sugars: 12g; Protein: 17g

## Garlicky Roasted Mushrooms

**Servings: 4 | Prep Time: 10 Minutes | Cooking Time: 30 Minutes**

### Ingredients:

- 16 garlic cloves, peeled
- 2 tsp olive oil
- 16 button mushrooms
- 2 tbsp fresh chives, snipped
- Salt and pepper to taste
- 1 tbsp white wine

### Directions:

1. Preheat air fryer to 175°C/350°F. Coat the garlic with some olive oil in a baking pan, then Roast in the air fryer for 12 minutes. When done, take the pan out and stir in the mushrooms, salt, and pepper. Then add the remaining olive oil and white wine. Put the pan back into the fryer and Bake for 10-15 minutes until the mushrooms and garlic soften. Sprinkle with chives and serve warm.

### Variations & Ingredients Tips:

- Use a variety of mushrooms like cremini, portobello or oyster for different flavors.
- Add a splash of balsamic vinegar or lemon juice before serving.
- Toss in fresh herbs like thyme or rosemary.

**Per Serving:** Calories: 90; Total Fat: 4g; Saturated Fat: 0.5g; Sodium: 10mg; Total Carbs: 12g; Dietary Fiber: 2g; Total Sugars: 1g; Protein: 3g

## Lentil Fritters

**Servings: 9 | Prep Time: 10 Minutes | Cooking Time: 12 Minutes**

### Ingredients:

- 1 cup cooked red lentils
- 1 cup riced cauliflower
- ½ medium zucchini, shredded (about 1 cup)
- ¼ cup finely chopped onion
- ¼ teaspoon salt
- ¼ teaspoon black pepper
- ½ teaspoon garlic powder
- ¼ teaspoon paprika
- 1 large egg
- ⅓ cup quinoa flour

### Directions:

1. Preheat the air fryer to 190°C/370°F.
2. In a large bowl, mix the lentils, cauliflower, zucchini, onion, salt, pepper, garlic powder, and paprika. Mix in the egg and flour until a thick dough forms.
3. Using a large spoon, form the dough into 9 large fritters.
4. Liberally spray the air fryer basket with olive oil. Place the fritters into the basket, leaving space around each fritter so you can flip them.
5. Cook for 6 minutes, flip, and cook another 6 minutes.
6. Remove from the air fryer and repeat with the remaining fritters. Serve warm with desired sauce and sides.

### Variations & Ingredients Tips:

- Use chickpea flour or almond meal instead of quinoa flour for a different flavor.
- Add shredded carrots or chopped bell peppers for extra veggie goodness.
- Serve with yogurt dip, hummus, or sweet chili sauce.

**Per Serving:** Calories: 60; Total Fat: 1.5g; Saturated Fat: 0g; Sodium: 90mg; Total Carbohydrates: 8g; Dietary Fiber: 2g; Total Sugars: 1g; Protein: 3g

## Healthy Living Mushroom Enchiladas

**Servings: 4 | Prep Time: 20 Minutes | Cooking Time: 40 Minutes**

### Ingredients:

- 2 cups sliced mushrooms
- ½ onion, thinly sliced
- 2 garlic cloves, minced
- 1 tbsp olive oil
- 280 grams spinach, chopped
- ½ tsp ground cumin
- 1 tbsp dried oregano
- 1 tsp chili powder
- ¼ cup grated feta cheese
- ¼ tsp red pepper flakes
- 1 cup grated mozzarella cheese
- 1 cup sour cream
- 2 tbsp mayonnaise
- Juice of 1 lime
- Salt and pepper to taste
- 8 corn tortillas
- 1 jalapeño pepper, diced
- ¼ cup chopped cilantro

### Directions:

1. Preheat air fryer to 200°C/400°F.
2. Combine mushrooms, onion, oregano, garlic, chili powder, olive oil, and salt in a small bowl until well coated. Transfer to the greased air fryer basket. Cook for 5 minutes, then shake the basket. Cook for another 3 to 4 minutes, then transfer to a medium bowl.
3. Wipe out the air fryer basket. Take the garlic cloves from the mushroom mixture and finely mince them. Return half of the garlic to the bowl with the mushrooms. Stir in spinach, cumin, red pepper flakes, and ½ cup of mozzarella.
4. Place the other half of the minced garlic in a small bowl along with sour cream, mayonnaise, feta, the rest of the mozzarella, lime juice, and black pepper.
5. To prepare the enchiladas, spoon 2 tablespoons of mushroom mixture in the center of each tortilla. Roll the tortilla and place it seam-side down in the baking dish. Repeat for the rest of the tortillas.
6. Top with sour cream mixture and garnish with jalapeños. Place the dish in the air fryer basket and bake for 20 minutes until heated through and just brown on top.
7. Top with cilantro. Serve.

### Variations & Ingredients Tips:

- Substitute mushrooms with zucchini, eggplant, or bell peppers for different veggie options.
- Use flour tortillas instead of corn tortillas for a softer texture.
- Add black beans, corn, or rice to the filling for extra heartiness.

**Per Serving:** Calories: 450; Cholesterol: 55mg; Total Fat: 31g; Saturated Fat: 13g; Sodium: 620mg; Total Carbohydrates: 34g; Dietary Fiber: 6g; Total Sugars: 7g; Protein: 16g

Total Sugars: 4g; Protein: 9g

## Mushroom Bolognese Casserole

**Servings: 4 | Prep Time: 10 Minutes | Cooking Time: 20 Minutes**

### Ingredients:

- 1 cup canned diced tomatoes
- 2 garlic cloves, minced
- 1 tsp onion powder
- ¾ tsp dried basil
- ¾ tsp dried oregano
- 1 cup chopped mushrooms
- 454 grams cooked spaghetti

### Directions:

1. Preheat air fryer to 200°C/400°F.
2. Whisk the tomatoes and their juices, garlic, onion powder, basil, oregano, and mushrooms in a baking pan. Cover with aluminum foil and Bake for 6 minutes.
3. Slide out the pan and add the cooked spaghetti; stir to coat. Cover with aluminum foil and Bake for 3 minutes until and bubbly.
4. Serve and enjoy!

### Variations & Ingredients Tips:

- Use zucchini noodles or spaghetti squash instead of regular pasta for a low-carb option.
- Add plant-based ground meat substitute for a meatier texture and more protein.
- Top with grated Parmesan cheese or nutritional yeast before serving.

**Per Serving:** Calories: 240; Total Fat: 1.5g; Saturated Fat: 0g; Sodium: 60mg; Total Carbohydrates: 49g; Dietary Fiber: 3g;

## Honey Pear Chips

**Servings: 4 | Prep Time: 10 Minutes | Cooking Time: 30 Minutes**

### Ingredients:

- 2 firm pears, thinly sliced
- 1 tbsp lemon juice
- ½ tsp ground cinnamon
- 1 tsp honey

### Directions:

1. Preheat air fryer to 190°C/380°F.
2. Arrange the pear slices on the parchment-lined cooking basket. Drizzle with lemon juice and honey and sprinkle with cinnamon.
3. Air Fry for 6-8 minutes, shaking the basket once, until golden.
4. Leave to cool. Serve immediately or save for later in an airtight container. Good for 2 days.

### Variations & Ingredients Tips:

- Substitute pears with apples or peaches for different flavors.
- Add a pinch of nutmeg or ginger for extra warmth and spice.
- Serve with a dollop of yogurt or ice cream for a sweet treat.

**Per Serving:** Calories: 70; Total Fat: 0g; Saturated Fat: 0g; Sodium: 0mg; Total Carbohydrates: 18g; Dietary Fiber: 3g; Total Sugars: 13g; Protein: 0g

# Desserts And Sweets

## Giant Buttery Oatmeal Cookie

**Servings: 4 | Prep Time: 15 Minutes | Cooking Time: 16 Minutes**

### Ingredients:

- 1 cup Rolled oats (not quick-cooking or steel-cut oats)
- ½ cup All-purpose flour
- ½ teaspoon Baking soda
- ½ teaspoon Ground cinnamon
- ½ teaspoon Table salt
- 3½ tablespoons Butter, at room temperature
- ⅓ cup Packed dark brown sugar
- 1½ tablespoons Granulated white sugar
- 3 tablespoons (or 1 medium egg, well beaten) Pasteurized egg substitute, such as Egg Beaters
- ¾ teaspoon Vanilla extract
- ⅓ cup Chopped pecans
- Baking spray

### Directions:

1. Preheat the air fryer to 180°C/350°F.
2. Stir the oats, flour, baking soda, cinnamon, and salt in a bowl until well combined.

3. Using an electric hand mixer at medium speed, beat the butter, brown sugar, and granulated white sugar until creamy and thick, about 3 minutes, scraping down the inside of the bowl occasionally. Beat in the egg substitute or egg (as applicable) and vanilla until uniform.
4. Scrape down and remove the beaters. Fold in the flour mixture and pecans with a rubber spatula just until all the flour is moistened and the nuts are even throughout the dough.
5. For a small air fryer, coat the inside of a 15-cm round cake pan with baking spray. For a medium air fryer, coat the inside of an 18-cm round cake pan with baking spray. And for a large air fryer, coat the inside of a 20-cm round cake pan with baking spray. Scrape and gently press the dough into the prepared pan, spreading it into an even layer to the perimeter.
6. Set the pan in the basket and air-fry undisturbed for 16 minutes, or until puffed and browned.
7. Transfer the pan to a wire rack and cool for 10 minutes. Loosen the cookie from the perimeter with a spatula, then invert the pan onto a cutting board and let the cookie come free. Remove the pan and reinvert the cookie onto the wire rack. Cool for 5 minutes more before slicing into wedges to serve.

### Variations & Ingredients Tips:

- Use quick oats or old-fashioned oats for a chewier texture.
- Add ½ cup of raisins, dried cranberries, or chocolate chips to the dough.
- Sprinkle with a mixture of cinnamon and sugar before baking for extra flavor.

**Per Serving:** Calories: 430; Total Fat: 22g; Saturated Fat: 8g; Sodium: 400mg; Total Carbohydrates: 54g; Dietary Fiber: 4g; Total Sugars: 25g; Protein: 7g

## Strawberry Donut Bites

**Servings: 6 | Prep Time: 10 Minutes | Cooking Time: 25 Minutes**

### Ingredients:

- 2/3 cup flour
- A pinch of salt
- 1/2 tsp baking powder
- 1 tsp vanilla extract
- 2 tbsp light brown sugar
- 1 tbsp honey
- 1/2 cup diced strawberries
- 1 tbsp butter, melted
- 2 tbsp powdered sugar
- 2 tsp sour cream
- 1/4 cup crushed pretzels

### Directions:

1. Preheat air fryer at 165°C/325°F.
2. In a bowl, sift flour, baking powder, and salt.
3. Add in vanilla, brown sugar, honey, 2 tbsp of water, butter, and strawberries and whisk until combined.
4. Form dough into balls. Place the balls on a lightly greased pizza pan, place them in the frying basket, and Air Fry for 10-12 minutes.
5. Let cool onto a cooling rack for 5 minutes.
6. Mix the powdered sugar and sour cream in a small bowl, 1 tsp of sour cream at a time until you reach your desired consistency.
7. Gently pour over the donut bites. Scatter with crushed pretzels and serve.

### Variations & Ingredients Tips:

- Use other fresh or frozen berries instead of strawberries.
- Top with a cream cheese glaze.
- Roll in cinnamon-sugar before baking.

**Per Serving:** Calories: 135; Total Fat: 3g; Saturated Fat: 2g; Cholesterol: 10mg; Sodium: 105mg; Total Carbs: 25g; Dietary Fiber: 1g; Total Sugars: 10g; Protein: 2g

## Apple Dumplings

**Servings: 4 | Prep Time: 20 Minutes | Cooking Time: 25 Minutes**

### Ingredients:

- 1 Basic Pie Dough (see the following recipe)
- 4 medium Granny Smith or Pink Lady apples, peeled and cored
- 4 tablespoons sugar
- 4 teaspoons cinnamon
- 1/2 teaspoon ground nutmeg
- 4 tablespoons unsalted butter, melted
- 4 scoops ice cream, for serving

### Directions:

1. Preheat the air fryer to 165°C/330°F.
2. Bring the pie crust recipe to room temperature.
3. Place the pie crust on a floured surface. Divide the dough into 4 equal pieces. Roll out each piece to 0.6cm-thick rounds.
4. Place an apple onto each dough round. Sprinkle 1 tablespoon of sugar in the core part of each apple; sprinkle 1 teaspoon cinnamon and 1/8 teaspoon nutmeg over each. Place 1 tablespoon of butter into the center of each.
5. Fold up the sides and fully cover the cored apples.
6. Place the dumplings into the air fryer basket and spray with cooking spray. Cook for 25 minutes. Check after 14 minutes cooking; if they're getting too brown, reduce the heat to 160°C/320°F and complete the cooking.
7. Serve hot apple dumplings with a scoop of ice cream.

### Variations & Ingredients Tips:

- Use different apple varieties like Honeycrisp or Fuji.
- Add raisins or chopped nuts to the filling.
- Drizzle with caramel sauce before serving.

**Per Serving:** Calories: 375; Total Fat: 18g; Saturated Fat: 10g; Sodium: 195mg; Total Carbohydrates: 51g; Dietary Fiber: 4g; Total Sugars: 29g; Protein: 3g

## Guilty Chocolate Cookies

**Servings: 6 | Prep Time: 10 Minutes | Cooking Time: 25 Minutes**

### Ingredients:

- 3 eggs, beaten
- 1 tsp vanilla extract
- 1 tsp apple cider vinegar
- 1/3 cup butter, softened
- 1/3 cup sugar
- ¼ cup cacao powder
- ¼ tsp baking soda

### Directions:

1. Preheat air fryer to 150°C/300°F.
2. Combine eggs, vanilla extract, and apple vinegar in a bowl until well combined. Refrigerate for 5 minutes.
3. Whisk in butter and sugar until smooth, finally toss in cacao powder and baking soda until smooth.
4. Make balls out of the mixture. Place the balls onto the parchment-lined air fryer basket.
5. Bake for 13 minutes until brown.
6. Using a fork, flatten each cookie. Let cool completely before serving.

### Variations & Ingredients Tips:

- Add chocolate chips, chopped nuts, or dried fruit to the dough for extra texture.
- Use coconut sugar or maple syrup instead of regular sugar for a healthier option.
- Serve with a glass of cold milk or a scoop of vanilla ice cream.

**Per Serving:** Calories: 220; Total Fat: 14g; Saturated Fat: 8g; Sodium: 140mg; Total Carbohydrates: 20g; Dietary Fiber: 2g; Total Sugars: 15g; Protein: 5g

## Donut Holes

**Servings: 13 | Prep Time: 15 Minutes | Cooking Time: 12 Minutes**

### Ingredients:

- 6 tablespoons Granulated white sugar
- 1½ tablespoons Butter, melted and cooled
- 2 tablespoons (or 1 small egg, well beaten) Pasteurized egg substitute, such as Egg Beaters
- 6 tablespoons Regular or low-fat sour cream (not fat-free)
- ¾ teaspoon Vanilla extract
- 1⅔ cups All-purpose flour
- ¾ teaspoon Baking powder
- ¼ teaspoon Table salt
- Vegetable oil spray

### Directions:

1. Preheat the air fryer to 180°C/350°F.
2. Whisk the sugar and melted butter in a medium bowl until well combined. Whisk in the egg substitute or egg, then the sour cream and vanilla until smooth. Remove the whisk and stir in the flour, baking powder, and salt with a wooden spoon just until a soft dough forms.
3. Use 2 tablespoons of this dough to create a ball between your clean palms. Set it aside and continue making balls: 8 more for the small batch, 12 more for the medium batch, or 17 more for the large one.
4. Coat the balls in the vegetable oil spray, then set them in the basket with as much air space between them as possible. Even a fraction of 0.25 cm will be enough, but they should not touch. Air-fry undisturbed for 12 minutes, or until browned and cooked through. A toothpick inserted into the center of a ball should come out clean.
5. Pour the contents of the basket onto a wire rack. Cool for at least 5 minutes before serving.

### Variations & Ingredients Tips:

- Toss the warm donut holes in cinnamon sugar or powdered sugar.
- Add grated lemon or orange zest to the batter for a citrusy flavor.
- Fill the donut holes with jam, Nutella, or pastry cream using a piping bag.

**Per Serving:** Calories: 130; Total Fat: 5g; Saturated Fat: 3g; Sodium: 100mg; Total Carbohydrates: 20g; Dietary Fiber: 0g; Total Sugars: 9g; Protein: 2g

## Almond-roasted Pears

**Servings: 4 | Prep Time: 10 Minutes | Cooking Time: 15 Minutes**

### Ingredients:

- Yogurt Topping
- 1 container (142-170g) vanilla Greek yogurt
- 1/4 teaspoon almond flavoring
- 2 whole pears
- 1/4 cup crushed Biscoff cookies (approx. 4 cookies)
- 1 tablespoon sliced almonds
- 1 tablespoon butter

### Directions:

1. Stir almond flavoring into yogurt and set aside while preparing pears.
2. Halve each pear and spoon out the core.
3. Place pear halves in air fryer basket.
4. Stir together the cookie crumbs and almonds. Place a quarter of this mixture into the hollow of each pear half.
5. Cut butter into 4 pieces and place one piece on top of crumb mixture in each pear.
6. Cook at 180°C/360°F for 15 minutes or until pears have cooked through but are still slightly firm.
7. Serve pears warm with a dollop of yogurt topping.

### Variations & Ingredients Tips:

- Use honey Greek yogurt instead of vanilla.
- Substitute graham cracker crumbs for Biscoff cookies.
- Drizzle with honey or maple syrup before serving.

**Per Serving:** Calories: 207; Total Fat: 8g; Saturated Fat: 3g; Sodium: 52mg; Total Carbohydrates: 31g; Dietary Fiber: 4g; Total Sugars: 20g; Protein: 5g

## Pear And Almond Biscotti Crumble

**Servings: 6 | Prep Time: 15 Minutes | Cooking Time: 65 Minutes**

### Ingredients:

- 18-cm cake pan or ceramic dish
- 3 pears, peeled, cored and sliced
- 1/2 cup brown sugar
- 1/4 teaspoon ground ginger
- 1 teaspoon ground cinnamon
- 1/8 teaspoon ground nutmeg
- 2 tablespoons cornstarch
- 1 1/4 cups (4 to 5) almond biscotti, coarsely crushed
- 1/4 cup all-purpose flour
- 1/4 cup sliced almonds
- 1/4 cup butter, melted

### Directions:

1. Combine the pears, brown sugar, ginger, cinnamon, nutmeg and cornstarch in a bowl. Toss to combine and then pour the pear mixture into a greased 18-cm cake pan or ceramic dish.
2. Combine the crushed biscotti, flour, almonds and melted butter in a medium bowl. Toss with a fork until the mixture resembles large crumbles. Sprinkle the biscotti crumble over the pears and cover the pan with aluminum foil.
3. Preheat the air fryer to 175°C/350°F.
4. Air-fry at 175°C/350°F for 60 minutes. Remove the aluminum foil and air-fry for an additional 5 minutes to brown the crumble layer.
5. Serve warm.

### Variations & Ingredients Tips:

- Use apples or a mix of pears and apples for the fruit base.
- Substitute brown sugar with maple syrup or honey.
- Add spices like cardamom or star anise to the crumble topping.

**Per Serving:** Calories: 340; Total Fat: 15g; Saturated Fat: 5g; Cholesterol: 20mg; Sodium: 125mg; Total Carbs: 50g; Dietary Fiber: 5g; Total Sugars: 28g; Protein: 5g

## Fruity Oatmeal Crisp

**Servings: 6 | Prep Time: 15 Minutes | Cooking Time: 25 Minutes**

### Ingredients:

- 2 peeled nectarines, chopped
- 1 peeled apple, chopped
- 1/3 cup raisins
- 2 tbsp honey
- 1/3 cup brown sugar
- 1/4 cup flour
- 1/2 cup oatmeal
- 3 tbsp softened butter

### Directions:

1. Preheat air fryer to 190°C/380°F.
2. Mix together nectarines, apple, raisins, and honey in a baking pan. Set aside.
3. Mix brown sugar, flour, oatmeal and butter in a medium bowl until crumbly.
4. Top the fruit in a greased pan with the crumble.
5. Bake until bubbly and the topping is golden, 10-12 minutes.
6. Serve warm and top with vanilla ice cream if desired.

### Variations & Ingredients Tips:

- Use different fruits like peaches, plums, berries, or pears.
- Substitute honey with maple syrup or agave nectar.
- Add chopped nuts like almonds, pecans, or walnuts to the crumble topping.

**Per Serving:** Calories: 250; Total Fat: 8g; Saturated Fat: 5g; Sodium: 65mg; Total Carbohydrates: 45g; Dietary Fiber: 3g; Total Sugars: 32g; Protein: 2g

## Chewy Coconut Cake

**Servings: 6 | Prep Time: 15 Minutes | Cooking Time: 18-22 Minutes**

### Ingredients:

- 3/4 cup plus 2 1/2 tablespoons All-purpose flour
- 3/4 teaspoon Baking powder
- 1/8 teaspoon Table salt
- 7 1/2 tablespoons (1 stick minus 1/2 tablespoon) Butter, at room temperature
- 1/3 cup plus 1 tablespoon Granulated white sugar
- 5 tablespoons Packed light brown sugar
- 5 tablespoons Pasteurized egg substitute, such as Egg Beaters
- 2 teaspoons Vanilla extract
- 1/2 cup Unsweetened shredded coconut
- Baking spray

### Directions:

1. Preheat air fryer to 165°C/325°F (or 170°C/330°F).
2. Mix flour, baking powder and salt.
3. Beat butter, white sugar and brown sugar until creamy, 3 mins.
4. Beat in egg substitute/egg and vanilla until smooth.
5. Fold in flour mixture just until moistened. Fold in coconut.
6. Grease a 15cm, 18cm or 20cm round cake pan with baking

spray.
7. Spread batter evenly into pan.
8. Air fry for 18 mins (15cm), 20 mins (18cm), 22 mins (20cm) until set in center.
9. Cool in pan 1 hour, then slice into wedges.

### Variations & Ingredients Tips:

- Use sweetened shredded coconut for extra sweetness.
- Add lime or orange zest to the batter.
- Top with coconut buttercream frosting.

**Per Serving:** Calories: 334; Total Fat: 17g; Saturated Fat: 10g; Sodium: 134mg; Total Carbohydrates: 42g; Dietary Fiber: 1g; Total Sugars: 23g; Protein: 4g

## Keto Cheesecake Cups

**Servings: 6 | Prep Time: 10 Minutes | Cooking Time: 10 Minutes**

### Ingredients:

- 225-g cream cheese
- 1/4 cup plain whole-milk Greek yogurt
- 1 large egg
- 1 teaspoon pure vanilla extract
- 3 tablespoons monk fruit sweetener
- 1/4 teaspoon salt
- 1/2 cup walnuts, roughly chopped

### Directions:

1. Preheat the air fryer to 155°C/315°F.
2. Beat the cream cheese with yogurt, egg, vanilla, sweetener and salt until combined.
3. Fold in the chopped walnuts.
4. Fill 6 silicone muffin liners with the batter. Place in an air fryer pan.
5. Carefully put the pan in the air fryer basket and cook for 10 minutes until lightly browned.
6. Refrigerate the cheesecake cups for 3 hours before serving.

### Variations & Ingredients Tips:

- Use other keto-friendly sweeteners like erythritol or stevia.
- Add lemon or orange zest to the batter.
- Top with fresh berries or sugar-free chocolate syrup.

**Per Serving:** Calories: 205; Total Fat: 18g; Saturated Fat: 9g; Sodium: 166mg; Total Carbohydrates: 4g; Dietary Fiber: 1g; Total Sugars: 2g; Protein: 6g

## Mango-chocolate Custard

**Servings: 4 | Prep Time: 15 Minutes | Cooking Time: 40 Minutes**

### Ingredients:

- 4 egg yolks
- 2 tbsp granulated sugar
- 1/8 tsp almond extract
- 1 1/2 cups half-and-half
- 3/4 cup chocolate chips
- 1 mango, pureed
- 1 mango, chopped
- 1 tsp fresh mint, chopped

### Directions:

1. Beat egg yolks, sugar and almond extract. Set aside.
2. Warm half-and-half in a saucepan until simmering.
3. Whisk some half-and-half into egg mixture, then whisk egg mixture into saucepan.
4. Stir in chocolate chips and mango puree for 10 mins until melted.
5. Divide custard into 4 ramekins.
6. Preheat air fryer to 175°C/350°F.
7. Bake ramekins for 6-8 minutes.
8. Cool, then chill in fridge for 2 hours up to 2 days.
9. Serve topped with chopped mango and mint.

### Variations & Ingredients Tips:

- Use coconut milk instead of half-and-half.
- Add a splash of rum or orange liqueur.
- Top with toasted coconut or crushed cookies.

**Per Serving:** Calories: 350; Total Fat: 21g; Saturated Fat: 11g; Sodium: 62mg; Total Carbohydrates: 35g; Dietary Fiber: 3g; Total Sugars: 27g; Protein: 7g

## Blueberry Crisp

**Servings: 6 | Prep Time: 10 Minutes | Cooking Time: 13 Minutes**

### Ingredients:

- 3 cups Fresh or thawed frozen blueberries
- 1/3 cup Granulated white sugar
- 1 tablespoon Instant tapioca
- 1/3 cup All-purpose flour
- 1/3 cup Rolled oats (not quick-cooking or steel-cut)
- 1/3 cup Chopped walnuts or pecans
- 1/3 cup Packed light brown sugar
- 5 tablespoons plus 1 teaspoon (2/3 stick) Butter, melted and cooled
- 3/4 teaspoon Ground cinnamon
- 1/4 teaspoon Table salt

### Directions:

1. Preheat the air fryer to 200°C/400°F.
2. Mix the blueberries, granulated sugar, and instant tapioca in a 15cm, 18cm or 20cm round cake pan.
3. Set the pan in the basket and air-fry for 5 minutes, until blueberries begin to bubble.
4. Meanwhile, mix flour, oats, nuts, brown sugar, butter, cinnamon, and salt in a bowl.
5. When blueberries bubble, crumble flour mixture evenly on top.
6. Continue air-frying for 8 minutes until topping is

browned and filling is bubbling.
7. Transfer pan to a wire rack and cool at least 10 minutes before serving.

### Variations & Ingredients Tips:

- Use other berries like raspberries or blackberries.
- Add lemon or orange zest to the crisp topping.
- Serve warm with a scoop of vanilla ice cream.

**Per Serving:** Calories: 322; Total Fat: 15g; Saturated Fat: 6g; Sodium: 122mg; Total Carbohydrates: 45g; Dietary Fiber: 3g; Total Sugars: 25g; Protein: 4g

## Sugared Pizza Dough Dippers With Raspberry Cream Cheese Dip

**Servings: 10 | Prep Time: 20 Minutes | Cooking Time: 8 Minutes**

### Ingredients:

- 450-g pizza dough
- 1/2 cup butter, melted
- 3/4 to 1 cup sugar
- 113-g cream cheese, softened
- 2 tablespoons powdered sugar
- 1/2 teaspoon almond extract or almond paste
- 1 1/2 tablespoons milk
- 1/4 cup raspberry preserves
- Fresh raspberries

### Directions:

1. Cut the ingredients in half or save half of the dough for another recipe.
2. When ready, remove pizza dough from fridge at least 1 hour before baking and let sit covered on counter.
3. Roll dough into two 38cm logs. Cut each into 20 slices and roll each 8-9cm long. Cut each in half and twist halves 3-4 times.
4. Place twisted dough on sheet, brush with melted butter and sprinkle with sugar.
5. Preheat air fryer to 175°C/350°F.
6. Brush basket with butter. Air-fry dough twists in batches of 8-12.
7. Air-fry 6 mins. Turn, brush other side with butter and air-fry 2 more mins.
8. Make dip while cooking: Whip cream cheese. Add powdered sugar, extract/paste and milk; beat smooth. Fold in preserves.
9. After cooking batches, place in dish and brush/coat generously with more butter and sugar.
10. Serve warm dippers with raspberry dip, garnished with fresh raspberries.

### Variations & Ingredients Tips:

- Use cinnamon-sugar coating instead of plain sugar.
- Add citrus zest to cream cheese dip.
- Serve with chocolate or caramel sauce for dipping.

**Per Serving:** Calories: 330; Total Fat: 16g; Saturated Fat: 10g; Cholesterol: 45mg; Sodium: 320mg; Total Carbs: 43g; Dietary Fiber: 1g; Total Sugars: 17g; Protein: 5g

## Holiday Peppermint Cake

**Servings: 4 | Prep Time: 10 Minutes | Cooking Time: 20 Minutes**

### Ingredients:

- 1 1/2 cups flour
- 3 eggs
- 1/3 cup molasses
- 1/2 cup olive oil
- 1/2 cup almond milk
- 1/2 tsp vanilla extract
- 1/2 tsp peppermint extract
- 1 tsp baking powder
- 1/2 tsp salt

### Directions:

1. Preheat air fryer to 190°C/380°F.
2. Whisk the eggs and molasses until smooth.
3. Slowly mix in olive oil, almond milk, vanilla and peppermint extracts.
4. In another bowl, sift together flour, baking powder and salt.
5. Gradually incorporate dry ingredients into wet ingredients until combined.
6. Pour batter into a greased baking pan and place in air fryer basket.
7. Bake for 12-15 minutes until a toothpick inserted comes out clean.
8. Serve and enjoy!

### Variations & Ingredients Tips:

- Use coconut or vegetable oil instead of olive oil.
- Add crushed peppermint candies or chocolate chips to the batter.
- Top with peppermint frosting or whipped cream.

**Per Serving:** Calories: 538; Total Fat: 27g; Saturated Fat: 4g; Sodium: 307mg; Total Carbohydrates: 67g; Dietary Fiber: 2g; Total Sugars: 28g; Protein: 8g

## Famous Chocolate Lava Cake

**Servings: 4 | Prep Time: 10 Minutes | Cooking Time: 15 Minutes**

### Ingredients:

- ¼ cup flour
- 1 tbsp cocoa powder
- ⅛ tsp salt
- ½ tsp baking powder
- 1 tsp vanilla extract
- ¼ cup raw honey
- 1 egg, beaten
- 2 tbsp olive oil
- 2 tbsp icing sugar, to dust

### Directions:

1. Preheat air fryer to 190°C/380°F.

2. Sift the flour, cocoa powder, salt, vanilla, and baking powder in a bowl.
3. Add in honey, egg, and olive oil and stir to combine.
4. Divide the batter evenly among greased ramekins.
5. Put the filled ramekins inside the air fryer and Bake for 10 minutes.
6. Remove the lava cakes from the fryer and slide a knife around the outside edge of each cake.
7. Turn each ramekin upside down on a saucer and serve dusted with icing sugar.

### Variations & Ingredients Tips:

- Add a tablespoon of instant coffee or espresso powder to the batter for a mocha flavor.
- Top with fresh berries, whipped cream, or a scoop of vanilla ice cream.
- Use dark chocolate chunks instead of cocoa powder for a richer taste.

**Per Serving:** Calories: 250; Total Fat: 12g; Saturated Fat: 2g; Sodium: 230mg; Total Carbohydrates: 34g; Dietary Fiber: 1g; Total Sugars: 26g; Protein: 4g

## Sweet Potato Pie Rolls

**Servings: 3 | Prep Time: 15 Minutes | Cooking Time: 8 Minutes**

### Ingredients:

- 6 Spring roll wrappers
- 1½ cups Canned yams in syrup, drained
- 2 tablespoons Light brown sugar
- 1/4 teaspoon Ground cinnamon
- 1 Large egg, well beaten
- Vegetable oil spray

### Directions:

1. Preheat the air fryer to 200°C/400°F.
2. Set a spring roll wrapper on a clean, dry work surface. Scoop up 1/4 cup of the pulpy yams and set along one edge of the wrapper, leaving 5cm on each side of the yams.
3. Top the yams with about 1 teaspoon brown sugar and a pinch of ground cinnamon.
4. Fold the sides of the wrapper perpendicular to the yam filling up and over the filling, partially covering it. Brush beaten egg over the side of the wrapper farthest from the yam.
5. Starting with the yam end, roll the wrapper closed, ending at the part with the beaten egg that you can press gently to seal. Lightly coat the roll on all sides with vegetable oil spray.
6. Set it aside seam side down and continue filling, rolling, and spraying the remaining wrappers in the same way.
7. Set the rolls seam side down in the basket with as much air space between them as possible. Air-fry undisturbed for 8 minutes, or until crisp and golden brown.
8. Use a nonstick-safe spatula and perhaps kitchen tongs for balance to gently transfer the rolls to a wire rack. Cool for at least 5 minutes or up to 30 minutes before serving.

### Variations & Ingredients Tips:

- Use fresh baked sweet potatoes instead of canned.
- Add pecans or walnuts to the filling.
- Drizzle with maple syrup before serving.

**Per Serving:** Calories: 275; Total Fat: 3g; Saturated Fat: 0.5g; Cholesterol: 50mg; Sodium: 240mg; Total Carbs: 58g; Dietary Fiber: 4g; Total Sugars: 24g; Protein: 4g

## Banana-lemon Bars

**Servings: 6 | Prep Time: 15 Minutes | Cooking Time: 40 Minutes**

### Ingredients:

- 3/4 cup flour
- 2 tbsp powdered sugar
- 1/4 cup coconut oil, melted
- 1/2 cup brown sugar
- 1 tbsp lemon zest
- 1/4 cup lemon juice
- 1/8 tsp salt
- 1/4 cup mashed bananas
- 1 3/4 tsp cornstarch
- 3/4 tsp baking powder

### Directions:

1. Mix flour, powdered sugar and melted coconut oil. Refrigerate.
2. Combine brown sugar, zest, juice, salt, bananas, cornstarch and baking powder.
3. Preheat air fryer to 175°C/350°F. Oil a baking pan.
4. Remove crust from fridge and press into bottom of pan. Air fry 5 mins until firm.
5. Spread lemon-banana filling over crust.
6. Bake for 18-20 mins until top is golden.
7. Cool completely before cutting into bars.

### Variations & Ingredients Tips:

- Use gingersnap crumbs in the crust.
- Substitute lime juice and zest for lemon.
- Top with toasted coconut before baking.

**Per Serving:** Calories: 252; Total Fat: 10g; Saturated Fat: 7g; Sodium: 165mg; Total Carbohydrates: 39g; Dietary Fiber: 2g; Total Sugars: 20g; Protein: 2g

## Chocolate Cake

**Servings: 8 | Prep Time: 10 Minutes | Cooking Time: 20 Minutes**

### Ingredients:

- 1/2 cup sugar
- 1/4 cup flour, plus 3 tablespoons
- 3 tablespoons cocoa

- 1/2 teaspoon baking powder
- 1/2 teaspoon baking soda
- 1/4 teaspoon salt
- 1 egg
- 2 tablespoons oil
- 1/2 cup milk
- 1/2 teaspoon vanilla extract

### Directions:

1. Preheat air fryer to 165°C/330°F.
2. Grease and flour a 15x15cm baking pan.
3. In a bowl, stir together sugar, flours, cocoa, baking powder, soda and salt.
4. Add egg, oil, milk and vanilla. Beat with a whisk until smooth.
5. Pour batter into prepared pan.
6. Bake at 330°F for 20 minutes until toothpick inserted comes out clean.

### Variations & Ingredients Tips:

- Add chocolate chips or chopped nuts to the batter.
- Substitute buttermilk for a moister cake.
- Top with chocolate frosting or powdered sugar.

**Per Serving:** Calories: 149; Total Fat: 4g; Saturated Fat: 1g; Sodium: 158mg; Total Carbohydrates: 26g; Dietary Fiber: 1g; Total Sugars: 14g; Protein: 3g

## Fried Twinkies

**Servings: 6 | Prep Time: 20 Minutes | Cooking Time: 5 Minutes**

### Ingredients:

- 2 Large egg white(s)
- 2 tablespoons Water
- 1½ cups (about 255 grams) Ground gingersnap cookie crumbs
- 6 Twinkies
- Vegetable oil spray

### Directions:

1. Preheat the air fryer to 200°C/400°F.
2. Set up and fill two shallow soup plates or small pie plates on your counter: one for the egg white(s), whisked with the water until foamy; and one for the gingersnap crumbs.
3. Dip a Twinkie in the egg white(s), turning it to coat on all sides, even the ends. Let the excess egg white mixture slip back into the rest, then set the Twinkie in the crumbs. Roll it to coat on all sides, even the ends, pressing gently to get an even coating. Then repeat this process: egg white(s), followed by crumbs. Lightly coat the prepared Twinkie on all sides with vegetable oil spray. Set aside and coat each of the remaining Twinkies with the same double-dipping technique, followed by spraying.
4. Set the Twinkies flat side up in the basket with as much air space between them as possible. Air-fry for 5 minutes, or until browned and crunchy.
5. Use a nonstick-safe spatula to gently transfer the Twinkies to a wire rack. Cool for at least 10 minutes before serving.

### Variations & Ingredients Tips:

- Substitute gingersnaps with graham crackers, shortbread cookies, or vanilla wafers.
- Fill the Twinkies with jam, peanut butter, or chocolate ganache before coating.
- Dust with powdered sugar or drizzle with honey before serving.

**Per Serving:** Calories: 340; Total Fat: 15g; Saturated Fat: 4.5g; Sodium: 270mg; Total Carbohydrates: 48g; Dietary Fiber: 1g; Total Sugars: 30g; Protein: 3g

## Holiday Pear Crumble

**Servings: 4 | Prep Time: 15 Minutes | Cooking Time: 40 Minutes**

### Ingredients:

- 2 tbsp coconut oil
- 1/4 cup flour
- 1/4 cup demerara sugar
- 1/8 tsp salt
- 2 cups finely chopped pears
- 1/2 tbsp lemon juice
- 3/4 tsp cinnamon

### Directions:

1. In a bowl, mix together coconut oil, flour, sugar and salt until crumbly.
2. Preheat air fryer to 160°C/320°F.
3. Stir together pears, 3 tbsp water, lemon juice and cinnamon in a baking pan.
4. Sprinkle chilled topping evenly over the pear mixture.
5. Bake for 30 minutes until pears are softened and topping is crispy.
6. Serve warm.

### Variations & Ingredients Tips:

- Use apples or a mix of fruits instead of just pears.
- Add oats, nuts or spices like nutmeg to the crumble topping.
- Drizzle with caramel sauce before serving.

**Per Serving:** Calories: 233; Total Fat: 9g; Saturated Fat: 5g; Sodium: 58mg; Total Carbohydrates: 38g; Dietary Fiber: 4g; Total Sugars: 23g; Protein: 2g

# INDEX

## A

Almond-roasted Pears   64
Apple Dumplings   63
Apricot-cheese Mini Pies   3
Artichoke-spinach Dip   29
Asian-style Shrimp Toast   28
Asparagus Fries   40
Asparagus, Mushroom And Cheese Soufflés   56
Avocado Fries With Quick Salsa Fresca   29

## B

Bacon Puff Pastry Pinwheels   3
Banana-lemon Bars   68
Barbecue-style Beef Cube Steak   23
Barbecue-style London Broil   17
Basil Crab Cakes With Fresh Salad   12
Beef Steak Sliders   26
Black Bean Stuffed Potato Boats   55
Black Bean Veggie Burgers   51
Blueberry Crisp   66
Broccoli Au Gratin   43
Buttered Swordfish Steaks   15
Buttery Stuffed Tomatoes   45

## C

Cajun-seasoned Shrimp   10
Canadian-style Rib Eye Steak   17
Cheddar & Sausage Tater Tots   5
Cheesy Egg Popovers   5
Cheesy Zucchini Chips   29
Chewy Coconut Cake   65
Chia Seed Banana Bread   5
Chicago-style Turkey Meatballs   33
Chicken Apple Brie Melt   46
Chicken Breasts Wrapped In Bacon   31
Chicken Club Sandwiches   53
Chicken Gyros   49
Chicken Meatballs With A Surprise   32
Chicken Pigs In Blankets   32
Chicken Salad With Roasted Vegetables   32
Chicken Saltimbocca Sandwiches   54
Chicken Skewers   33
Chicken Souvlaki Gyros   34
Chicken Spiedies   47
Chili Cheese Dogs   46
Chili Hash Browns   6
Chinese-style Lamb Chops   18
Chocolate Cake   68
Cholula Onion Rings   42
Chorizo & Veggie Bake   19
Cinnamon Banana Bread With Pecans   4
Cinnamon Biscuit Rolls   8
Classic Beef Meatballs   23
Coconut Chicken With Apricot-ginger Sauce   35
Coconut-shrimp Po' Boys   10
Colorful French Toast Sticks   8
Country Wings   28
Crab Toasts   29
Creamy Broccoli & Mushroom Casserole   56
Crispy "fried" Chicken   37
Crispy Chicken Parmesan   38
Crispy Pierogi With Kielbasa And Onions   20
Crispy Sweet-and-sour Cod Fillets   11
Crunchy Falafel Balls   52

## D

Dijon Roasted Purple Potatoes   41
Dijon Thyme Burgers   50
Donut Holes   64

## E

Egg And Sausage Crescent Rolls   6
Eggplant Parmesan Subs   47

## F

Falafel   58
Famous Chocolate Lava Cake   67
Favorite Fried Chicken Wings   34
Fennel & Chicken Ratatouille   34
Fiery Cheese Sticks   28
Fish And "chips"   13
Fish Tacos With Jalapeño-lime Sauce   14
Flounder Fillets   16

French Grouper Nicoise   13
Fried Eggplant Balls   44
Fried Twinkies   69
Fried" Pickles With Homemade Ranch   27
Fruity Oatmeal Crisp   65

## G

Garlicky Brussels Sprouts   43
Garlicky Roasted Mushrooms   60
German Chicken Frikadellen   36
Giant Buttery Oatmeal Cookie   62
Gorgeous Jalapeño Poppers   57
Greek Pork Chops   19
Greek Street Tacos   30
Grits Casserole   41
Guilty Chocolate Cookies   64

## H

Hawaiian Brown Rice   40
Healthy Living Mushroom Enchiladas   61
Herby Parmesan Pita   7
Holiday Pear Crumble   69
Holiday Peppermint Cake   67
Home-style Fish Sticks   15
Honey Donuts   9
Honey Mesquite Pork Chops   21
Honey Pear Chips   62
Honey-roasted Parsnips   45
Hot Avocado Fries   26

## I

Inside Out Cheeseburgers   53
Inside-out Cheeseburgers   54
Italian Breaded Eggplant Rounds   40

## J

Jerk Chicken Drumsticks   39

## K

Keto Cheesecake Cups   66

## L

Lamb Chops   17
Lamb Meatballs With Quick Tomato Sauce   20
Lemony Green Bean Sauté   40
Lentil Fritters   61
Lime Halibut Parcels   11

Lime Muffins   4

## M

Mango-chocolate Custard   66
Maple Bacon Wrapped Chicken Breasts   38
Mascarpone Iced Cinnamon Rolls   3
Mediterranean Granola   7
Mediterranean Potato Skins   25
Mediterranean Roasted Vegetables   44
Mexican Cheeseburgers   49
Morning Loaded Potato Skins   8
Mushroom & Cavolo Nero Egg Muffins   5
Mushroom Bolognese Casserole   62

## N

Nutty Shrimp With Amaretto Glaze   14

## O

Oat & Nut Granola   7
Original Köttbullar   23

## P

Parmesan Pizza Nuggets   31
Party Giant Nachos   55
Peachy Pork Chops   22
Pear And Almond Biscotti Crumble   65
Perfect Burgers   52
Perfect Soft-shelled Crabs   15
Philly Cheesesteak Sandwiches   54
Philly Chicken Cheesesteak Stromboli   35
Pineapple & Veggie Souvlaki   60
Pinto Bean Casserole   58
Polenta Fries With Chili-lime Mayo   30
Pork Cutlets With Aloha Salsa   22
Pork Tenderloin With Apples & Celery   24
Pretzel-coated Pork Tenderloin   18
Prosciutto Polenta Rounds   27
Provolone Stuffed Meatballs   48

## R

Rigatoni With Roasted Onions, Fennel, Spinach And Lemon Pepper Ricotta   59
Roasted Garlic And Thyme Tomatoes   42
Roasted Peppers With Balsamic Vinegar And Basil   45
Roasted Vegetable Pita Pizza   58
Roasted Veggie Bowls   59

Roman Artichokes   44

## S

Salmon Burgers   48
Saucy Shrimp   11
Sausage And Pepper Heros   52
Sausage-cheese Calzone   21
Shrimp Al Pesto   12
Sloppy Joes   19
Southern-fried Chicken Livers   37
Speedy Shrimp Paella   13
Spiced Nuts   26
Spicy Black Bean Turkey Burgers With Cumin-avocado Spread   36
Spicy Chicken And Pepper Jack Cheese Bites   25
Spicy Fish Street Tacos With Sriracha Slaw   12
Spicy Fried Green Beans   43
Spicy Sesame Tempeh Slaw With Peanut Dressing   57
Spinach & Turkey Meatballs   36
Strawberry Donut Bites   63
Stuffed Pork Chops   18
Sugared Pizza Dough Dippers With Raspberry Cream Cheese Dip   67
Super Crunchy Flounder Fillets   10
Sweet Potato Pie Rolls   68
Sweet Potato–wrapped Shrimp   15
Sweet-and-salty Pretzels   24

## T

Tender Steak With Salsa Verde   22
Thai Turkey And Zucchini Meatballs   33
Thai Turkey Sausage Patties   9
Thanksgiving Turkey Sandwiches   48
Thyme Lentil Patties   56
Tilapia Al Pesto   16
Toasted Choco-nuts   41
Tomato & Garlic Roasted Potatoes   24
Tri-color Frittata   4
Tuna Platter   42

## V

Vegetarian Paella   60
Vietnamese Gingered Tofu   59

## W

White Bean Veggie Burgers   51

## Z

Zucchini Fries   39
Zucchini Fritters   27

Printed in Dunstable, United Kingdom